Healing the Past

Catholic Anti-Semitism:

Roots and Redemption

Healing the Past

Catholic Anti-Semitism:
Roots and Redemption

ENA GRAY

VERITAS

To the Jewish people, the children of Abraham,
Isaac and Jacob

In gratitude, for all we owe them, and in an effort to undo
some of the harm we have inflicted on them

'I am delighted to recommend Ena's book. As a catechist I found it a worthwhile read and I feel this informative book has much to offer those who wish to deepen their knowledge of the subject.'

Linda Quigley
(former National Director of Catechetics for the Catholic Bishops of
Ireland)

'Ena Gray has written an honest, well-documented assessment of the process of anti-Semitism and injustice across centuries, throughout Europe, with the Jewish people as victims. Hopefully, this work will be adopted in our colleges and seminaries, so that the widespread ignorance of the topic will be addressed. Let us pray that the perspectives presented in the final chapter, "Repentance, Redemption, Hope", will incrementally promote a new awareness of the need to respect the People of the Book.'

Dr Jacob Pearlmann (former Chief Rabbi of Ireland)

'The declaration on the Relationship of the Church to non-Christian Religions of the Second Vatican Council states: "The Church ... mindful of her common patrimony with the Jews ... deplores the hatred, persecutions and displays of anti-Semitism directed against the Jews at any time and from any source (4)." Sadly, Christians have been agents of anti-Semitism down though the centuries. Happily, there are many signs that Catholics are taking the teaching of the Council seriously. Ena Gray's book is one of those signs. Any Catholic who is interested in the history of the difficult relationship between the Church and the Jews – and that ought to be every committed member of the Church – should read *Healing the Past*.'

Bishop William Murphy (Kerry)

'Such a short book cataloguing 2,000 years of lethally destructive prejudice has a shocking effect on the reader. It's like a sudden piercing light dispelling ignorance, leaving behind a strong desire to atone in some way.'

Eugene Boyle
(works in the field of reconciliation)

First published 2009 by
Veritas Publications
7/8 Lower Abbey Street
Dublin 1
Ireland
Email publications@veritas.ie
Website www.veritas.ie

ISBN 978 1 84730 165 9

10 9 8 7 6 5 4 3 2 1

Extracts from *Healing the Wounds of History*
by Monsignor Peter Hocken, courtesy of Goodnews, 2005.

A catalogue record for this book is available from the
British Library.

Cover designed by Lir Mac Cárthaigh

Printed in the Republic of Ireland
by ColourBooks Ltd, Dublin

Veritas books are printed on paper made from the wood
pulp of managed forests. For every tree felled, at least one
tree is planted, thereby renewing natural resources.

Contents

Foreword   11
Bishop Donal Murray

Introduction   15

CHAPTER ONE   The Fathers of the Church and
                   Anti-Semitism   17

CHAPTER TWO   The Middle Ages – The Crusades,   39
                   The Inquisition

CHAPTER THREE   The Ghettos – Italy, Poland, Russia   67

CHAPTER FOUR   From the Ghetto to the Birth
                   of Zionism   81

CHAPTER FIVE   The Holocaust – Participators and
                   Collaborators   92

CHAPTER SIX   Ireland and the Jews   112

CHAPTER SEVEN   Repentance, Redemption, Hope   129

APPENDICES   Extract from Obituary of
                   Sr Rose Thering OP   145

Extracts from
Healing the Wounds of History
by Monsignor Peter Hocken   147

Acknowledgements   156

Foreword

The history of the relationship between Christians and Jews tells of tragic and inexcusable events and attitudes in which people betrayed the principles of their own Christian faith. It is clear that there is no limit to the love of neighbour preached by Jesus. Those who participated in the many atrocities and injustices against Jewish people and those who did not intervene when they could have done so, betrayed their own humanity. Many such events are documented in this book and they make sad reading.

The twentieth century saw the most unspeakable of these tragedies. As that century came to an end the Catholic Church said:

> We cannot know how many Christians in countries occupied or ruled by the Nazi powers or their allies were horrified at the disappearance of their Jewish neighbours and yet were not strong enough to raise their voices in protest. For Christians, this heavy burden of conscience of their brothers and sisters during the Second World War must be a call to penitence ...
>
> This is an act of repentance (*teshuva*), since, as members of the Church, we are linked to the sins as well as the merits of all her children ... It is not a matter of mere words, but indeed of binding

> commitment ... We would risk causing the victims of the most atrocious deaths to die again if we do not have an ardent desire for justice, if we do not commit ourselves to ensure that evil does not prevail over good as it did for millions of the children of the Jewish people ... Humanity cannot permit all that to happen again.[1]

Ena Gray has provided material for reflection which will call the readers to implement that 'binding commitment'. Each member of the Church needs to hear the call. Each of us is part of the 'we' who must 'have an ardent desire for justice', who must 'commit ourselves to ensure that evil does not prevail over good as it did for millions of Jewish people'.

There is a further horror involved in anti-Semitism when it is perpetrated by Christians. It is a denial of who we are. Mary and the Apostles were Jews; the New Testament opens with the genealogy of Jesus, showing him as a descendent of Abraham and David (Mt 1:1-17); we reverence the Hebrew Scriptures, which we call the Old Testament, as the Word of God. When a young man asks what he must do to inherit eternal life Jesus begins by quoting the Commandments 'which express the implications of belonging to God' through the Covenant with Moses.[2] The central act of our liturgy originated in the Paschal Meal celebrated by Jesus with his disciples before his death, when he said, 'Do this in remembrance of me' (Lk 22:19).

The late Cardinal Jean Marie Lustiger, himself a Jew, pointed to the challenge that exists in a world of diverse cultures:

---

1 Commission for Religious Relations with the Jews, *We Remember: A Reflection on the Shoah* IV, V, 1998.
2 Mt 19:16-19, cf. *Catechism of the Catholic Church*, 2062.

> At the risk of losing itself in losing its universality, Christianity cannot accept being separated from its roots in Israel, that is to say separated from the Covenant, the first choice of God. The meeting, the link, of Jews and Christians, in the tension of respecting each other, offers the whole of humanity the original face of God and strengthens its hope of peaceful unity.[3]

Christians and Jews share the revelation of the God of Abraham. They await the coming of a Messiah, but in different ways, since Christians believe that he has come for the first time and wait for him to come again. No true Christianity can exist without its Jewish roots.

The relationship between us must respect the diversity of our different perspectives. Both the particularity of God's irrevocable choice of his people and the universality of the mission to bring God's revelation to the nations are vital to the richness of God's self-communication to humanity. Cardinal Lustiger as a Christian saw himself as still engaged in the vocation of Israel in 'bringing light to the goyim'. He composed the wording of a plaque to be erected in his cathedral, Notre Dame: 'I was born Jewish. I received my paternal grandfather's name, Aaron, I became Christian by faith and baptism, and I remained Jewish like the Apostles did.'

I hope that this book will help to raise awareness of the evil of prejudice and in particular the evil of anti-Semitism. When Pope John XXIII received a group of Jewish people in audience, he greeted them with the words: 'I am Joseph your brother.' When Pope Benedict XVI visited the Synagogue in

---

3   J.M. Lustiger, Conference for 25th anniversary of *Nostra aetate*, Rome, 27 October 2005.

Cologne he finished his address with a prayer, a Jewish prayer, which should be the prayer of all who read this book: 'I conclude with the words of Psalm 29, which express both a wish and a prayer: "May the Lord give strength to his people, may he bless his people with peace."'[4]

+Donal Murray
March 2009

4   Benedict XVI, Synagogue of Cologne, 19 August 2005.

Introduction

In 2003 Pope John Paul II called on all Catholics to make every effort possible to build friendships with Jews:

> It is necessary to encourage dialogue with Judaism ... that acknowledgement be given to any part which the children of the Church have had in the growth and spread of anti-Semitism in history; forgiveness must be sought for this from God, and every effort must be made to favour encounters of reconciliation and of friendship with the sons of Israel.[1]

The idea of writing a short account of the history of Catholic anti-Semitism came to me from a personal experience. While spending a short time in Israel in 2000, I was surprised when a Jewish lady made a chance reference to the persecution of Jews in the Middle Ages. I asked myself, 'What does she mean?' I had taught history myself and had studied European history in some depth but I had no recollection of any significant persecution of the Jewish people. I asked myself if I had been so indifferent that I had paid no attention to the subject, or could it be that there was actually no reference to it in my studies?

---

1   The Apostolic Exhortation of Pope John Paul II, 'Ecclesia in Europa', 2003.

I began to look around and found a book by the Jewish scholar Dan Cohn Sherbok entitled *The Crucified Jew: Twenty Centuries of Christian Anti-Semitism*. What I read there both shocked and saddened me: the wanton slaughter of Jews by crusaders supposedly en route to free the Holy Places in Palestine, the preposterous libels which led to torture and burnings, etc. Next I went in search of an authoritative Catholic source and found *The Anguish of the Jews* by Monsignor Edward Flannery. This book confirmed all that Dr Cohn had said, and more. Significantly also, Flannery, in the introduction to the second edition of his book (1980), makes the comment that 'the vast majority of Christians, even well educated, are all but totally ignorant of what happened to the Jews in history' and of what he calls the 'culpable involvement of the Church'. I could identify with this statement and I then realised that I was not alone. It was not that my memory had failed me or that I had been too indifferent to notice – there actually had been no reference to the subject either in my school years or in my degree course. It seemed to me that this was not only a grave injustice to the Jewish people but that it also had serious implications for the continuing problem of anti-Semitism worldwide.

It appeared therefore, in the context of our need for reconciliation, that it would be useful to make a short account of this story available to Catholics generally and to busy priests and catechists in particular. It is my hope that this account of how the Catholic Church was involved in causing pain, death and destruction to our 'elder brothers and sisters' over the centuries will help the reader to see the need for the 'encounters of reconciliation and friendship with the sons of Israel' of which Pope John Paul II spoke. Much of it makes difficult and unpleasant reading, but is necessary, I believe, if there is to be reconciliation and if we are to fully appreciate the extraordinary change that has taken place in our own Church in the last forty years, and the hope that this augurs for us all.

CHAPTER ONE

The Fathers of the Church and Anti-Semitism

> The Schism within the Judeo-Christian tradition
> has been generated by intense feelings of betrayal
> on both sides. It was inevitably more bitter than
> the conflicts of Christians with other religions. It
> is an unresolved and irresolvable quarrel within
> the family.[1]

On the occasion of the celebration of the fortieth anniversary
of the promulgation of the decree *Nostra aetate* in Rome,
Rabbi David Rosen made this statement: 'These forty years
since the promulgation of *Nostra aetate* have seen a remarkable
reckoning of the soul on the part of the Church and its
rediscovery of its unique relationship with Judaism and the
Jewish people ...' He concluded his address with the following
adaptation of a Jewish prayer: 'Thanks to the One Lord,
Creator and Sovereign of the Universe who has preserved us
in life so that we may reach this day, to praise him for his Spirit
manifest in this historic transformation that we celebrate
tonight.'[2] Already that same year (2005), a group of
prominent rabbis and politicians had visited the late Pope to

1   Norman Davies, *Europe: A History*, London: Pimlico, 1997, p. 197.
2   '*Nostra aetate*: Present and Future Perspectives', address by Rabbi David
    Rosen. Conference of the Holy See Commission for Religious Relations
    with Jewry, Rome, 27 October 2005.

thank him for all his work for the Jewish people. On that occasion Rabbi Jack Bemporad made this statement: 'In the history of the world, the last forty years will be seen as the most revolutionary and significant in terms of progress in the Jewish-Catholic relationship.'[3]

However, awareness of this 'transformation' in our Church is confined to a small minority. This brief account of the story behind these hope-filled developments is intended to highlight and clarify the extraordinary events that are happening in our own day, and to encourage us to participate fully in them.

The Story of the Jewish-Christian Schism (c.35–135)

The first Christian Pentecost marks the birthday of the Christian Church. On the day of Pentecost the task of preaching the Good News began and as a result, scriptures tell us, 'about three thousand people were added to the group' (Acts 2:41). We assume that Peter and the other apostles expected that this was just the beginning, and that soon all their fellow Jews would acknowledge Jesus as the promised Messiah. But, of course, the reality was quite different. This initial success was soon followed by the murder of Stephen, and shortly afterwards Saul set out on his mission to persecute the followers of Jesus.

There were many different groups within the Jewish fold at the time of Jesus and the apostles. The only one of these groups to survive the Destruction of the Temple and the Fall of Jerusalem, in the long term, was the Pharisees. Therefore their difficulties about the claim that Jesus was the Messiah concern us in a particular way. The picture they had of the Promised Messiah was given to them by one of their own rabbis only a century before. This profile is contained in

3   Quoted in *Alive!* (free newspaper), February 2005.

Psalm 17 of a collection of psalms called the Psalms of Solomon:

> He will be ... a Son of David, an anointed of the Lord. He will rid the nation of its enemies and restore Jerusalem, making it holy as of old ... His weapon is the word of his mouth ... as a righteous king taught by God and pure from sin, he is Judge and Shepherd. He destroys sinners and drives out the Gentiles. Thereby he gathers together a holy people and he shall not suffer unrighteousness to dwell in their midst for all shall be holy.[4]

Many of the Pharisees of Jesus' time could not see how this prophecy was fulfilled in him. The nation was not rid of its enemies, the Gentiles had not been driven out and there was manifestly plenty of unrighteousness about. As teachers of the Law, it was also their firm belief that the call of every Jew was to obey the will of God as revealed in the Torah. In their zeal to effect the conversion of Judaism, which they believed to have been unfaithful, they had taken on themselves the task of practising the standards of purity required by the Temple priesthood in their entirety, hoping that by so doing they would achieve the perfect observance of the Law. But the followers of Jesus claimed that faith in Jesus was the source of salvation, and not the Law (Rom 7:6). To the Pharisee, this was equivalent to rejecting the Law altogether – the ultimate apostasy. This was also the problem Paul faced before his conversion.[5]

Apart from the Pharisees, there were also a number of apocalyptic sects within Judaism. These sects believed that

---

4 'Paul, Christ, Society and the Church', lecture by Fr Jerome Murphy O'Connor OP, Tallaght, September 2003, Éist Audio Recording Services, Dublin.
5 Ibid.

official Judaism was unfaithful to the Covenant at Sinai to the point of apostasy. The fact that the Jews were constantly at the mercy of great and powerful empires was evidence to them of God's displeasure. Therefore, sects such as the Zealots, the Essenes and others called their followers to be converted and to accept baptism as a sign of that conversion. These would then become 'sons of light' who would fight with God in the final apocalyptic battle between the 'sons of light' and 'the sons of darkness'. It was one of these groups, the Zealots, that led the revolt against Rome in AD 69, a rebellion that brought the wrath of the Roman armies down on Jerusalem.

In this hour of need the Pharisees joined their fellow Jews in a supreme effort to defend the city and protect the Temple. The Christians (still Jews) took a different stance. Believing that this calamity was a fulfillment of the prophecy of Jesus that the temple would fall and that 'not a stone would be left upon a stone' (Mt 24:2), they withdrew to the other side of the Jordan and awaited the outcome. Unsurprisingly, their fellow Jews saw this as rank betrayal.

While they joined in the struggle, the Pharisees did not believe in the apocalyptic battle of the Zealots, and so they helped their leader, Rabbi Yocha Ben Zakkai, to escape. He secretly left the siege at Jerusalem and went to Javneh, where he founded a rabbinical school. This school developed the teaching that 'acts of repentance, thanksgiving, and loving kindness were equal to – or better than – Temple sacrifice', a teaching that was crucial in providing a way for Judaism to continue into the future.[6]

By the year 80, when the Gospel of Matthew was being compiled, new developments are apparent. This gospel includes negative references to 'the Jews'. Fr Raymond Brown, a scripture scholar, believes that these refer to those Jews who

---

6   Rosemary Radford Ruether, *Faith and Fratricide*, USA: Seabury, 1974, p. 53.

had now become the opponents of the Christians i.e. the Jews of 80, rather than the Jews of Jesus' own time. He concludes therefore that these references indicate that a separation of the ways was already taking place and a new religion beginning to emerge. He notes that Christians were now referring to their Jewish brothers as 'them' and talking of what 'they' did to 'our prophet', rather than, as they might have done in the past, speaking of what had been done to 'a' prophet e.g. Jeremiah.[7] Similarly Matthew 10:17 refers to *'their* synagogues'.

It was about this time too that the Sanhedrin in Javneh made the decree ordaining that all male Jews should recite a malediction against the 'minim', or heretics, three times daily. The wording of this malediction is as follows: 'May the minim perish in an instant; may they be effaced from the book of life and not be accounted among the just.' (There has been a lot of dispute about the meaning of 'minim' in this context but according to Flannery: 'All agree that the prayer was introduced to weed out Judaeo-Christians from synagogue services.'[8] This presumably refers to Christians teaching in synagogues, since it is clear that Christians often attended synagogue services long after this date, something that caused grave concern to their own leaders.)

7   Fr Raymond Browne, *An Introduction to the New Testament*, New York: Doubleday, 1997, pp. 39, 166–7. (According to the Vatican document 'The Jewish People and their Sacred Scriptures in the Christian Bible' (2001), references to 'the Jews' in John's gospel are generally imprecise in their meaning, but as the gospel is written in the context of the difficult relations between them, the reference is to those who were hostile – clearly it did not include all Jews, since John himself and the other believers were Jews. Sadly this distinction was not made as time went one, and dramatic presentations of the Passion were often the starting point for attacks on Jews.)
8   Monsignor Edward Flannery, *The Anguish of the Jews*, USA: Paulist Press, 1985, p. 32. See also note 8, p. 308.

At the beginning of the second century, another Jewish leader emerged also claiming to be the Messiah. His name was Shimon Bar Kokva. Bar Kokva led another revolt against the Romans with the support of the influential Rabbi Akiba and a majority of the Jews. As on the previous occasion, the Romans soon overcame this uprising, killing many Jews and selling many more into slavery, and in a determined effort to put an end to 'Jewish insubordination', they banished Jews from Jerusalem altogether in 135, devastated the entire land and renamed it Syria Palestina, with the intent of wiping out the memory of Judea forever.

The support given to this 'Messiah' made it clear to the Christian community that their hope of a mass conversion of their brothers to Jesus was now gone.

Dispersed throughout the Empire, the Pharisees engaged in missionary activity with greater vigour now than ever, determined to ensure the future of their Jewish faith. At the same time, Christian preachers strove to convert the pagan world to Christ. As both faiths shared common roots, it became necessary for each to prove the other wrong. A sizeable proportion of the writing of the Fathers of the Church is concerned with their side of the story and is found in the writings referred to as 'Adversus Judaeos': against the Jews. These writings draw upon the teaching of the apostles but they also go way beyond that teaching, becoming ever more negative as the tension between the two groups increased.

Apostolic Teaching

Prior to the Resurrection and Pentecost, the apostles themselves were more than confused by the fact that Jesus had died, and died on a cross. They had not taken on board Jesus' warnings about his impending death (cf. Lk 18:31-33), nor had they understood the many references to it in their scriptures (cf. Lk 24:25-27). Jesus' death therefore was not only a great personal loss, but also a shattering blow to their faith. In the aftermath of the Pentecost experience, Peter explained what had happened and what it meant: 'In accordance with his own plan, God had already decided that Jesus would be handed over to you, and you killed him by letting sinful men crucify him' (Acts 2:23). Peter has no doubt about where the burden of responsibility lay but he does not condemn. He says: 'And now my friends, I know that what you and your leaders did to Jesus was due to your ignorance ... Repent then and turn to God so that he will forgive your sins' (Acts 3:17ff).

Stephen also lays the responsibility for Jesus' death on fellow Jews and expands the idea further (Acts 7:2-53). In a brief résumé of the history of the people of Israel, he reminds those present of how the people of Israel had refused to obey Moses on so many occasions. He concludes with these words: 'How stubborn you are ... how deaf you are to God's message! You are just like your ancestors!' Stephen then identifies his accusers (members of the Jewish Sanhedrin who rejected Jesus as messiah) with all those Israelites who had refused to listen to God in the past. (Paul makes a similar equation in 1 Thessalonians 2:15 when he speaks of 'the Jews who killed the Lord Jesus and the prophets'.)

But both Peter and Stephen hold out hope of forgiveness, while Paul confirms his belief that God will never abandon his people:

> There is a secret truth, my friends, which I want you to know, for it will keep you from thinking how wise you are. It is that the stubbornness of the people of Israel is not permanent, but will last only until the complete number of Gentiles comes to God ... Because they reject the Good News, the Jews are God's enemies for the sake of you Gentiles. But because of God's choice, they

> are his friends because of their ancestors. For
> God does not change his mind about whom he
> chooses and blesses. (Rom 11:25ff)

Therefore Paul sees his fellow Jews as being cut off now because of their unbelief, but asserts that this is for the sake of us, the Gentiles. He goes on to remind us that we must not, however, think of ourselves as superior. They are the natural branches of God's olive tree, broken off for a time through unbelief in their Messiah, but able to be 'grafted back into their own olive tree' much more readily than Gentile Christians, who are grafted in as branches cut from a wild olive tree (cf. Rom 11:17-24). And he is confident that this will come about in God's time.

As we know from the Acts of the Apostles, Paul had quite a struggle in the course of his mission, and while it is clear that he always retained his love for his own people, sometimes he sees them in another light. In the letter to the Galatians he gives us an example of this:

> Let me ask those of you who want to be subject
> to the Law: do you not hear what the Law says? It
> says that Abraham had two sons, one by a slave
> woman, the other by a free woman. His son by a
> slave woman was born in the usual way, but his
> son by the free woman was born as the result of
> God's promise. These things can be understood
> as a figure: the two women represent two
> covenants. The one whose children are born in
> slavery is Hagar, and she represents the Covenant
> made at Mount Sinai ... (v.28) Now you, my
> friends are God's children as a result of his
> promise, just as Isaac was ... (v.31) ... we are not
> the children of a slave woman but of a free
> woman. (Gal 4:21-31)

It seems that the Fathers of the Church drew from this text the belief that the Christian Church has become the true heir of God's promise and from this developed the teaching known as 'replacement theology': the belief that the Old Covenant has been replaced by the New (represented by the Christian Church). This is in spite of the fact that Paul clearly teaches in Romans XI that God has not changed his mind about the Jews, nor has the plan he has for them.

Teaching of the Fathers of the Church (c.100–430)

The period of the Fathers of the Church stretches from the time of the Apostles to the death of St Augustine (430). Our concern here is with those preachers and teachers who clarified and defended the Christian faith up to and after the Council of Nicaea in 325. This includes the first great Doctors of the Church, such as St John Chrysostom, St Jerome and St Augustine.

The task these men faced was far from easy. Heresies, sects and schisms abounded and were always a cause of great concern. These divisions were sometimes accompanied even by violence and sharp disagreements amongst the preachers and teachers themselves. (Some of the 'Greats' such as St Hippolytus, who became an anti-Pope for a time, and Tertullian, who ended his days in a sect called the Montanists, are numbered in this revered company!)

St Justin Martyr was one of the first great teachers. Born in Samaria (c.100) of pagan parents, he founded a school in Rome some years after his conversion and is the author of a tract called 'Dialogue with Trypho' (a Jewish rabbi). The tract consists of a fictitious debate between the two. The tone of the work is friendly and both characters agree to pray for each other at the end of their discussion. However, Justin makes it quite clear that he believes his opponent to be entirely wrong. So clear, in fact, that he tells Trypho that the fall of Jerusalem and the dispersion of the Jews are 'tribulations [that] were justly imposed upon you, for you have murdered the Just One'.[9] This judgement marks a new and damning progression from earlier teaching. Not only does Justin place responsibility for the death of Jesus squarely on the shoulders of the Jews and their descendants, he adds his own personal conviction that God is now punishing them for this crime of their forebears. This position became the commonly accepted one after Justin and is repeated many times in the works of the Fathers who succeeded him.

Five years after Justin's death (165), St Hippolytus was born in Italy. He became a member of the Roman clergy and is reputed to have distinguished himself as the most important writer of the Roman Church in the third century.[10] His work, entitled *Demonstratio Adversus Judaeos*, makes similar assertions:

> Why was the temple made desolate? Was it on account of the ancient fabrication of the calf? Or was it on account of the idolatry of the people? Was it for the blood of the prophets? Was it for the adultery and fornication of Israel? By no means, for all these transgressions they always found pardon open to them. But it was because they killed the Son of their Benefactor, for he is co-eternal with the Father.[11]

9 Thomas Falls (trans.), *The Writings of Justin Martyr*, Fathers of the Catholic Church, Vol. 2, New York: Christian Heritage Inc., 1948.

10 *The New Catholic Encyclopedia*, Vol. 6, Washington DC: Catholic University of America Press, 2003.

11 *Demonstratio Adversus Judaeos*, St Hippolytus, Ante-Nicene Christian Literature, Lukyn Williams (trans.), Cambridge: Cambridge University Press, 1935.

Shortly after him (185), Origen was born in Egypt of Christian parents. He spent most of his life in Alexandria and was regarded as the greatest theologian and the most prolific biblical scholar in the Eastern Church, before the Council of Nicaea (325). His contribution is found in a work called *Contra Celsus*, a composition that also takes the form of a fictitious discussion. The opponent in this case is a pagan philosopher, Celsus, who argues the case for the Jews. Origen reiterates Justin's teaching, adding yet another element – permanence. Contradicting Romans 11:26, he says: '[T]heir rejection of Jesus has resulted in the present calamity and exile ... they will never be restored to their former condition because they committed a crime of the most unhallowed kind in conspiring against the Saviour of the human race.'[12]

The claim is often made by Christians that the Jews of this time displayed great hatred towards them. Much has been written on this subject and there is still disagreement about it. Whatever the truth may be however, one cannot help noting how lacking the Christian preachers were in their appreciation of why the Jews might be so angry. To the Jews it appeared that not only were the Christians both traitors and apostates, but they found their preaching deeply insulting. The Jews themselves believed also that they were being punished by God, but because of their infidelity to the Law of Moses, not because they had rejected Jesus. Furthermore it was an insult to their God to suggest that he had abandoned them and was therefore unfaithful to his promises. On the contrary they saw this punishment as sent by a loving God for their healing. They believed faithfully that God would never abandon his people. If this preaching wasn't bad enough and potentially damaging to their missionary effort (so urgent to them at that time), these preachers were using their own Hebrew scriptures to substantiate it.

12 *Contra Celsus*, Origen, ibid., Vol. 4.

Despite all these circumstances however, Jewish proselytising was actually having a lot of success at this point. This is explained, in part no doubt, by the fact that the ancient world had great respect for age and antiquity and was equally suspicious of all that was new or novel. The Jewish faith had a long history behind it. Competition was keen therefore, and so Christian leaders were particularly perturbed when they found that many of their converts, retaining a liking for Jewish customs and ceremonies, continued to attend Jewish synagogues, even when forbidden to do so. The Fathers referred to this practice as 'Judaising' and saw it as a serious threat to the new-found faith of Christians.

St John Chrysostom, whose homilies *Adversus Judaeos* are among the most offensive of all the anti-Semitic writings of the Fathers, was particularly disturbed by the 'judaising' practises of his flock. Born in Antioch, Syria (c.344), John ministered there before becoming Archbishop of Constantinople. This city had a large and prosperous Jewish community and Christians were in the habit of visiting their synagogues. In an attempt to address this issue John wrote the eight homilies of *Adversus Judaeos*, all of which have been recorded and preserved for posterity. In one he sets out the reasons for 'this combat' with the Jews:

> I too in the past frolicked about in explicating the
> Scriptures, as if I were sporting about in some
> meadow; I took no part in polemics because there
> was no one causing me concern. But today the
> Jews, who are more dangerous than any wolves,
> are bent on surrounding my sheep, so I will spur
> into them and fight with them so that no sheep
> of mine may fall victim to those wolves.[13]

13 St John Chrysostom, 'Discourses against Judaising Christians', Paul
   Harkins (trans.), *Discourse 4*, Catholic University Press of America, 1979.

True to his word, he launched into what is generally acknowledged to be the most abusive and highly offensive of verbal attacks ever made on the Jews. The following extracts are typical of these homilies:

> [The Jews are] inveterate murderers, destroyers, men possessed by the devil ... debauchery and drunkenness have given them the manners of the pig and the lusty goat ... Why are the Jews degenerate? Because of their odious assassination of Christ ... for this deicide there is no expiation possible, no indulgence, no pardon ... Christians may never cease to seek vengeance on the Jews and they must live in servitude forever ... God always hated the Jews and whoever has dealings with the Jews will be rejected on judgement day.[14]

While one cannot condone his language, in fairness to John, one finds that when these homilies are taken together, the overall impression is much more of his profound, even obsessional, concern for his own flock, rather than any preoccupation with the Jews. It is also true that in the polemics of the time many strong things were said on both sides. The Jewish rabbis had very negative and offensive things to say to Christians also. 'For them Jesus was a false messiah, a usurper, a renegade' and there were even suggestions that he was illegitimate and that his mother was a prostitute.[15]

The greatest problem with John's homilies is that because of the high esteem in which John was held, his works were treated with a great reverence and studied with great assiduity by clerics for centuries to come. Long after the context in

---

14 Ibid. Discourse 1 and 6.
15 Flannery, *The Anguish of the Jews*, p. 37.

which they were written had changed, their content could and would be applied on many occasions in an offensive and even dangerous way.

St Jerome (born c.342), a contemporary of John's, was also highly esteemed, being regarded as the most learned biblical scholar in the West. One of his major works was the translation of the Old Testament into Latin. He is said to have consulted with Jewish rabbis when working on this project and to have hired a Jewish scholar named Bar Ananias to teach him Hebrew. Jerome never wrote a specific work 'adversus Judaeos', but the references to Jews in his writings are negative e.g. 'serpents, haters of men, and Judases'.[16]

St Augustine was probably the best known and the best loved of the Fathers of the Church in the West. He was born in North Africa near the present Tunisian border in 354. He was baptised by St Ambrose in Italy (387), and consecrated bishop of Hippo in 396, after his return to his native Africa. The story of Augustine's episcopacy is remarkable for the number and nature of the difficulties he faced, and no less for the compassion with which he approached these problems. His teaching concerning the Jews is all the more mystifying on that account.

Augustine equates all Jews with Judas. This may be a play on words, as the name Judas also means Jew, but, like his predecessors, he blames them for the killing of Christ. He writes that they must not be killed, because they are, he says, 'slave librarians' of the Church, as it were, and as such must remain as witnesses to evil and to Christian truth. Augustine also strongly emphasises another aspect of anti-Semitic teaching which, though not new then either, had all the greater influence on the tradition because of his extraordinary standing in the Christian community. He

16 Ibid., p. 50. See also notes 12–15, p. 306.

derived this teaching from the story of Jacob and Esau. He writes:

> How is it true that the elder shall serve the younger when the younger seems to worship the elder? But these things were not accomplished in history that they may be understood as prophecies relating to the future. The younger son took the birthright, and the elder lost it. Jacob has filled the earth, he has conquered peoples and kingdoms. The Roman Emperor, himself a Christian, commanded that the Jews should not go up even to Jerusalem. Scattered over the earth, they have become, as it were, the keepers of our books. Like servants, who, when they go to their lord's audience, carry their documents, and sit outside, so has it been with the eldest son in regard to the youngest.[17]

This 'servant role' applied to the Jews by Augustine and others was adhered to quite rigidly by successive popes and bishops who repeatedly insisted that Christian rulers must not afford honours or privileges to Jews and that Jews must not be allowed to occupy roles which give them precedence over Christians.

Augustine also maintained that since Jacob represented the Church and Esau Judaism, the era of the Covenant of Sinai was now over and the Christian Church replaced it as 'the chosen people of God' – the 'replacement theology' rejected by Vatican II in the decree *Nostra aetate*.

17 Mary H. Allies, 'Jacob and Esau in the Church' (Sermons IV and V), *Leaves from St Augustine*, London: Washbourne, 1899, pp. 324–6.

The Growth of the Church's Political Power (c.300-800)

By 300, the Christian community had become the largest religious community in the Empire. Constantine I, son of St Helena, chose to align himself with this community in his struggle to control the Empire. (He postponed his baptism until on his deathbed, a practice not uncommon at the time.) Crowned Emperor in 305, he passed the Edict of Milan in 313, which granted toleration to all cults in the Empire. Ten years later he granted 'a place of special favour' to the Christian Church. As part of a campaign to promote unity in the Church and in the Empire, he convened the Council of Nicaea in 325, giving the delegates the task of summarising the basic tenets of Christian belief. After his death, but almost certainly at his behest (his sons were preoccupied with the struggle for succession), the imperial government began the process of withdrawing from the Jews all the privileges they had previously been allowed by the Roman Empire.

The Christian Church was now in the ascendant position, though as yet this situation was not stable. This is evidenced by the fact that Julian 'the Apostate' became emperor in 361. It is said that Julian was raised a Christian by Christians who had murdered his family. In any case he always declared himself an advocate of paganism. 'The end result was an edict of general toleration, and a last respite for the Roman gods.'[18] It is also said to have encouraged Christians to revert to Judaism and to have made known his plan to rebuild the Temple in Jerusalem. St Ambrose refers to this in a letter to Theodosius: 'Have you not heard how, when Julian had ordered the Temple of Jerusalem rebuilt, those who were clearing the rubbish were burned by fire from heaven.'[19]

18 Davies, *Europe: A History*, p. 259.
19 Sr Mary Melchior Beyenka OP (trans.), *St Ambrose Letters*, Fathers of the Christian Church, 1954, p. 10.

Later in that century the pagan population rose up in rebellion against the Christian Empire and were supported by the Jews, who burnt some Christian churches. In retaliation the Christians burned their synagogues, but this burning of synagogues continued a long time after the end of the rebellion. The imperial government passed six successive laws in an attempt to put a stop to it. Surprisingly (from our modern point of view), some Church leaders were unhappy with this decision. St Ambrose is a case in point. He expressed his position clearly in an interchange with the Emperor Theodosius over the instance of the burning of the synagogue in Callinicum, on the eastern frontier of the Empire. The local bishop there had led the mob responsible for the burning. Theodosius ordered that the synagogue be rebuilt and the culprit punished (378–395). St Ambrose (archbishop of Milan, d.397) promptly intervened, threatening to excommunicate Theodosius if he did not repeal the order. His reasons are given in a letter to Theodosius. He writes:

> Let no one call the bishop to task for performing his duty. [It had been suggested that a prince or count would repair it.] ... Will you, the Emperor, have the count an apostate? Shall a place be provided out of the spoils of the Church for the disbelief of the Jews? ... The maintenance of civil law should be secondary to religion.[20]

Clearly in the mind of Ambrose, the power of the State was at the service of the Christian Church. The consequence of this for the Jewish people was very serious.

A hundred years later, when Theodosius II (408–450) had all laws passed since Constantine I gathered together into the

20 Ibid.

Codex Theodosianus, we find that most of these laws related to the Jews. By then (1) it had become a criminal offence for Jews to seek converts; (2) those who did convert to Judaism were legally incapable of inheriting property; (3) regulations had been made governing the repair and beautification of synagogues; (4) the Jewish Patriarchate was abolished and the tax, formerly given to the Patriarch to pay for communication with his subjects in the diaspora, was passed to the State and became a head tax on all Jews; (5) Jews were barred from most public offices and any position giving them authority over Christians; (6) they were forbidden to buy Christian slaves (a regulation understandable from a Christian point of view, since Jewish law required that all members of a household, including slaves, to be circumcised, but the consequence for Jews was seriously damaging – the economy of the time was a slave economy and most available slaves were Christian, hence this law effectively ruled them out of the ownership of farms or industrial enterprises. Prior to this most Jews were involved in farming. Now they had to look elsewhere to make a living).

As a consequence of these developments, Jewish missionary activity had ceased altogether by the fifth century and the study of Torah had become both their focus and their refuge. Jewish scholars and scribes (first in Javneh, later in Babylon) had long since begun recording the oral traditions of commentary and law, and these writings, plus elaborations by famous rabbis, would eventually be collected together to form the Talmud.

One hundred years later again (550), when the Emperor Justinian came to power, he replaced the Codex Theodosianus with another (more severe) legal code. The Justinian Code took away from the Jews the right to legal assistance and protection and also imposed new regulations, some of which even concerned their forms of worship. The Jews reacted strongly to this treatment, and when the Persian army invaded 'the Land' (now Syria Palestina), they

34

supported the invaders. But the imperial army overcame the Persians and the Jews were punished very harshly. The Emperor Heraclius tried then to impose baptism on them. (This action had a precedent – Severus, the bishop of Minorca, in a letter 'ad omnem ecclesiam', gives an account of how he forced the baptism of all the Jews on that island in 418. The letter has been preserved.)[21] This attempt to force baptism on Jews was to recur many times in succeeding centuries. Frequently on such occasions the Jews, who saw it as apostasy to accept, preferred to take their own lives rather than submit.

St Gregory the Great became Latin Patriarch (later called Pope) in 590. He was a strong leader with great administrative ability and he took care of civil as well as religious affairs in Rome. (The Latin Patriarchs had managed to break free from political control.) Gregory initiated a policy of protection for the Jews, and his decree 'Sicut Judaeis' became a guideline for most of the popes of the Middle Ages. This decree affirmed the right of Jews to their possessions, their rituals and their synagogues. It also forbade Christians to vilify them, and on occasion Gregory himself personally intervened to protect Jews from violence and from efforts to force conversion on them. He is remembered in Jewish history as 'the first great papal friend of the Jews'.[22] Nevertheless, he made a distinction between civil rights and the religious position of the Jews, for when King Reccared of Spain sanctioned the decrees of the Council of Toledo, forbidding Jews to own Christian slaves, marry Christian women or hold public office, Gregory sent a letter to him praising him for his stand against the 'unbelief' of the Jews.

---

21 Radford Ruether, *Faith and Fratricide*, notes, p. 281.
22 Rabbi David C. Dalin, *The Myth of Hitler's Pope*, Washington DC: Regnery Publishing Inc., 2005, p. 20.

The Jews in Spain

King Reccared was a Visigoth and an Arian who converted to Catholicism in 587. Like so many other rulers, his ambition was to rule a monolithic kingdom where all his subjects worshipped the same God. So after his conversion, he initiated laws restricting the freedom of Jews. This policy was continued, with varying degrees of diligence, by his immediate successors until it reached the stage where Jewish rites were forbidden and the Jews themselves reduced to slavery. Sisebut (c.621) was the last of this line of kings and he tried to expel the Jews altogether by giving them the option of baptism or exile. But just at this point help came from outside, when in 711 the Muslim leader, Torik, invaded and overran the Iberian peninsula. Torik was welcomed by the Jewish community, and he, in turn, accepted them as his lawful subjects. The period that followed in Spain, when Muslim, Jew and Christian worked together, is regarded as a 'Golden Age' and is renowned for its enormous creativity and prosperity.

The Jews in Gaul (France)

The Muslim conquests of the seventh century cut off the old trade routes from Europe to India and China. This opened opportunities up for Jews in the north-west of the continent. Secular rulers there became aware that the Jews, who had been driven from the land of Judea in 135, were scattered throughout their own western kingdoms but there were also some who lived as far to the east as China. These rulers realised that these contacts plus the expertise which the Jews had acquired in the dispersion could be useful to provide links with their lost markets. They were very happy then to confer honours and privileges in return for such services.

Charlemagne was crowned Emperor of the Holy Roman Empire by Leo III in 800. He was particularly noted for the honour and privileges he conferred on Jews. St Agobard, bishop of Lyons, protested fiercely against this and the language he used has been compared to that of St John Chrysostom. Norman Davies comments that 'he did appear to believe that the Catholic Church was about to be invaded by Jews. When his collected works were discovered in 1605 it turned out that he had devoted no fewer than five treatises to the Jewish peril'.[23]

Agobard's anxiety was probably due in part to the fact that Bodo, court chaplain to Louis the Pious, had converted to Judaism, as had another eminent churchman, Andreas, Archbishop of Bari, about this time. But, whereas his objection to the honours given to Jews suggests that such conversions were motivated by ambition, there is evidence to suggest that there were other reasons. Corruption was widespread in the Church, while the Jewish community, by contrast, had managed to maintain a high standard of discipline and community living. The synagogue at Bari, in particular, had acquired a reputation for its standards of discipline and devotion. In relation to the comparison drawn between Agobard and St John Chrysostom, it is surely more than a coincidence that the only existing original manuscript of John's homilies are housed in a library in Paris named Codex Agobardinus or cod. Paris 1622. Clearly Agobard was a devotee of St John but it would appear that he failed to appreciate the difference in their respective contexts.

The teaching of the Fathers of the Church regarding Jews and Judaism was firmly established by the start of the early Middle Ages (c.800); that is to say, the 'roots of Catholic Anti-Semitism' had been established. This teaching was indeed a 'teaching of contempt', maintaining that all Jews were guilty of the death of Jesus, and had for that reason been abandoned

23 Davies, p. 304.

by God, replaced by the Christian Church as the 'chosen people of God', and forced to live out their lives as servants of the Church.

This teaching, which evolved from the arguments and tensions of the early Church, represents the claims of the victors in that debate. It was all too easy for Christians who, from the time of Constantine, wielded the political power, to interpret their triumph as the sign of God's approval. That they also saw their power as part of the victory of Christ is not so easy to understand, since Christ clearly stated that his 'kingdom was not of this world'. With the benefit of hindsight, this can only be seen as negative. The policy of Pope Gregory the Great and his successors to try and prevent violence against the Jews could not have succeeded in these circumstances. The core problem lay in the teaching itself, to which even Gregory subscribed.

CHAPTER TWO

The Middle Ages

No nation has ever suffered so much for God. Dispersed among the nations without king or secular ruler, the Jews are oppressed with heavy taxes as if they have to purchase their very lives every day. To mistreat the Jews is considered a deed pleasing to God ... The life of the Jews is in the hands of their worst enemies ... If they want to travel to the nearest town, they have to buy protection with high sums of money from the Christian rulers who actually wish for their death so that they can confiscate their possessions. The Jews cannot own land or vineyards because there is nobody to vouch for their safe-keeping. Thus, all that is left them as a means of livelihood is the business of money-lending, and this in turn brings the hatred of Christians upon them.[1]

THE CRUSADES

The phenomenon of Christian 'Holy Wars', or 'Wars of the Cross' as the crusades were called, cannot be excused, but in order to understand anything about them at all we must first look at the context out of which they came. On the one hand

1 Peter Abelard, the twelfth-century theologian, in Flannery, p. 142.

were the changes that had occurred in Europe prior to the new millennium, and on the other, the events outside the continent that contributed to this development.

The first fact of note is that the Roman Empire had disappeared and that the political separation between East and West was complete. Added to this is another fact: when first the Goths (and later the Lombards) invaded Italy in the fourth century, the Roman patriarchs were forced to seek protection from whatever source they could find. Pope Stephen II (752–7) and later Pope Leo III (795–816) were to turn to the kingdom of the Franks. It was Leo who eventually crowned Charlemagne emperor of 'the Holy Roman Empire' (800) and received in return not only the protection he needed, but also the territory which would later form the basis of the Papal States.

The result of these developments for the Jews was that the West now had its own empire, with its own *Christian* emperor, and in this new empire they were a very vulnerable minority. This vulnerability was soon to be exposed in the crusades against the so-called 'infidel'.

Outside of Europe the rise of Mahommed (seventh century) and the descent of the Seljuk Turks into Asia Minor (tenth century) paved the way for the 'Wars of the Cross'. The Seljuks embraced the Muslim religion with such enthusiasm that the names 'Turk' and 'Muslim' came to be synonymous. They brought with them an Islamic revival and this resulted in a renewed period of conquest. It was in the course of these wars that Caliph Hakim captured Jerusalem (1009), destroying the Church of the Holy Sepulchre and persecuting the Jews and Christians already there. (The first Muslim conquerors had permitted the return of the Jews to Jerusalem.) A shockwave passed through Christendom as news of these events spread abroad, partly because of the taking of the Holy Places, but perhaps even more because of the threat posed to Constantinople and even to Europe itself.

The Emperor of the East, Alexius, approached Pope Urban II with a request for military aid. The Pope did not actually have any troops, but he did have reason to get involved: (1) the Schism with the Eastern Church had come to a head in 1054 and the authorities in Rome were desperate to find a way to heal the breach. Urban hoped that if he could help Alexius and his people in their hour of crisis, this action might pave the way to reconciliation; (2) the constant warfare which accompanied the spread of feudalism had been a cause of great concern for some time and a 'solution' had been proposed in France (and supported by the monastery at Cluny where the Pope had been a monk), called 'the Truce of God'. The proposal was that a 'truce' allowing for the taking up of arms on certain days of the week and for certain good causes (such as protecting Church property or defending peasants) should be permitted. This idea then gave rise to the notion of taking up arms in a 'holy cause'. And so it was that on 17 November 1095, at a council convened at Clermont to extend 'the Truce of God' to the universal Church, Pope Urban surprised everyone by calling on Christians 'to engage in a War of the Cross for the deliverance of the Holy Sepulchre from the hands of the infidel'. It seems that the Pope in his turn was surprised by the extent and enthusiasm of the response. In fact the enthusiasm was such that not only did large crowds of knights set off, but large numbers of monks and peasants joined them, crying aloud, it is said: 'God wills it!'[2]

> The secret of success ... was in the taking up of the notion of pilgrimage ... The journey to Jerusalem had been the tacit desire of many Christians from time immemorial, it freed one

2 Hubert Jedin (ed.), *The History of the Church*, Vol. III, New York: Crossroad Publishing, 1980, pp. 449, 448.

> from all other penitential obligations ... But penitents who were pilgrims were not allowed to bear arms ... At the Council of Clermont, Urban granted the same full remission of canonical penalties that was gained by pilgrims to Jerusalem and therefore he proclaimed for the first time the idea of 'armed pilgrimage' ... the preaching of the Crusade it seems went further than this and was extended to mean a full plenary indulgence and 'a crude suggestion of forgiveness for sin' was probably also included.[3]

But this was not the whole story. Norman Davies gives another perspective: 'Religious fervour was mixed with the resentments of a society suffering from waves of famine, plague and overpopulation ... the well-fed knights with their well-shod retinues were far outnumbered by the hordes of paupers who followed in their wake.'[4] For the knights there was the hope of acquiring land; for all there was the prospect of booty. Christian merchants operating in the Mediterranean were interested in combating Muslim pirates who frequently attacked their ships.

In 1096 the First Crusade set out under the knightly leadership of Godfrey de Bouillon. There was no direct line of command and the knights were soon joined by a monk named Peter the Hermit, who recruited mobs of peasants – men, women and children – along the way. All were eager to embrace the challenge of taking up arms against the 'infidel'. This word 'infidel' takes its origin from the Latin word 'fides' meaning 'faith'. 'Fideles' denoted the 'faithful' or believers; subsequently 'infideles' were those who did not have 'faith' i.e. the unbelievers. But to the Christian mind at that time, the principal unbeliever, and the one they knew best, was the

3   Ibid.
4   Davies, p. 358c.

Jew. The chronicler Guibert of Nogent (1053–1124) reports these words attributed to the Crusaders of Rouen: 'We desire to combat the enemies of God in the East, but we have under our own eyes the Jews, a race more inimical to God than all the others. We are doing this thing backwards.'[5]

This was certainly not what Urban had in mind, but it was the interpretation the crusaders decided to accept. Jewish communities all along the Rhine from Rouen and Lorraine through Speyer, Worms, Mainz, Treves, Neuss and Ratisbon on into Bohemia and Prague, were suddenly attacked on all sides and without any warning by these crusaders who called on them to 'embrace the Cross or die'. Albert of Aix, a survivor of the attack on Mainz (May 1096), gives this eyewitness account of what happened in that city:

> The Jews of the city, knowing of the slaughter of their brethren, fled in hope of safety to the Bishop of Ruthard. They put an infinite treasure in his guard and trust, having much faith in his protection. He placed the Jews in a very spacious hall in his own house that they might remain safe and sound in a very secure and strong place.
>
> But ... the band held council, and after sunrise attacked the Jews in the hall with arrows and lances, breaking down the bolts in the doors. They killed the Jews, about 700 in number who in vain resisted the force of an attack of so many thousands. They killed the women also and with their sword pierced tender children whatever age and sex. The Jews, seeing that their Christian

5   Guiberti, De Vita Sua III, cited in Flannery, p. 91, 5 in PL (Latin version of the Fathers of the Church, 156:903), Paris: Garnier, 1878–1890.

enemies were attacking them and their children, and that they were sparing no age, likewise fell upon one another, brother, children, wives, and sisters, and thus they perished at each other's hands. Horrible to say, mothers cut the throats of the nursing children with knives and stabbed others, preferring them to perish thus by their own hands rather than be killed by the weapons of the uncircumcised.[6]

Lest one think that this is a biased view, another version by the Christian chronicler, Ekkard of Aurach (who claimed to have taken part in the crusades himself), reads as follows: 'In all the cities through which they went, they either completely exterminated or forced baptism on the remnants of the wicked Jews, those internal enemies of the Church. But very many of them returned to their former faith as the dog to his vomit.'[7]

Other Christian chroniclers give triumphant and bloodthirsty accounts of the slaughter that took place in Jerusalem. Most of those killed there were, of course, Muslim, but there were a significant number of Jews also. A Muslim chronicler, Ibn Al Qalinisi, gives us this information: '[T]he poor Jews had all huddled together in a synagogue and this is where the crusaders found them, set the place on fire, and burned them alive.'[8]

From a military point of view, the First Crusade was successful. Jerusalem was taken by the crusaders. But in 1144 the Turks began an attack to recover the lost ground, and there was an immediate cry for another crusade. Pope Eugene

---

6 August Krey, *The First Crusade: The Accounts of Eyewitnesses and Participants*, Princeton: Princeton University Press, 2001.

7 Jedin, *The History of the Church*, p. 605.

8 Rabbi Ken Spiro, 'Crash Course in Jewish History', accessed at www.aish.com/literacy/Jewish history. 2.2.09.

III called the Second Crusade in 1146. St Bernard was one of the main advocates of this crusade: 'Take up the sign of the Cross and you will find indulgence for all the sins which you confess ... Venture with devotion and the gain will be God's kingdom.'[9] However, mindful of the excesses of the earlier crusade, he did make serious efforts to prevent a repeat of those atrocities. Unfortunately, he was forestalled.

The trouble began when Radulph, a Benedictine monk who had absented himself from his monastery, went about preaching that Jews were the enemies of God and should therefore be persecuted. This man succeeded in rousing the mobs to turn on the Jews once more and neither the emperor nor the bishops were able to stop them. The Archbishop of Mainz appealed to Bernard for help, and in his response to the archbishop, Bernard accused Radulph of 'foolishness ... unauthorised preaching, contempt for episcopal authority and incitation to murder'. When all else failed, he confronted the monk in person and persuaded him to go back to his monastery.[10] But it was already too late. The Jews of Cologne, Speyer, Mainz, Wurzburg (Germany), and Carenton, Sully and Rameru (France) were attacked and the number of deaths is said to have reached several hundred. This crusade failed to recover the ground lost in the Middle East.

St Bernard's appeal that atrocities not be carried out against the Jews was genuine, a fact that has been acknowledged by Jewish historians. Nevertheless, his teaching (expressed in the above letter to the Archbishop of Mainz) presents the same negative message as the earlier Fathers:

> The Jews are not to be persecuted, killed or put to flight ... the Jews are for us the living word of Scripture, for they remind us always of what the

9   *Letters of St Bernard*, Anselm Biggs (trans.), London: Burns & Oates, 1980.
10 Ibid.

Lord has suffered. They are dispersed all over the world so that by expiating their crime they may be everywhere living witnesses of our redemption ... Under Christian princes they endure hard captivity, but they only wait for the time of their deliverance.[11]

The Turks recaptured Jerusalem in 1187, and Richard II of England (called 'Lion Heart') led the Third Crusade in another attempt to recapture the Holy City. He was joined by Philip II of France and Frederick Barbarossa of Germany. Frederick was persuaded 'financially' and 'diplomatically' on this occasion to issue a decree threatening dire punishment on anyone who injured a Jew. As a result Germany was spared the atrocities of the previous crusades. For England, however, this was the 'first' crusade and Richard's departure was the occasion for another massacre of Jews, this time in England, at Yorkminster. Here too, many Jews chose suicide rather than die at the hands of their attackers. It is significant, in terms of the motives for the attacks, that all records of debts due them were destroyed by the attackers.[12] (Richard made it clear on his return that he did not appreciate this – it involved a loss to the exchequer.) The Third Crusade failed in its objective also. Other minor crusades were undertaken from time to time until 1291, when the last of the crusader strongholds was captured by the Turks. All of the crusades were accompanied by attacks on Jews.

Aftermath of the Atrocities against the Jews

The murder and pillaging that occurred during the crusades horrified many people, as Davies records: 'The conduct of the crusaders was shocking – not only to modern sensibilities, but

11 Ibid.
12 Flannery, p. 119.

equally to contemporaries.'[13] And Flannery says: 'The massacres left a stunned Jewish population, and as the accounts of various chroniclers show, a troubled Christian conscience ... Strangely, in the wake of the massacres, popular hostility towards Jews increased and their social position suffered further deterioration.'[14] He concludes that, rather than deal with its troubled conscience, the Christian world chose to believe 'that the atrocities must have been deserved'.[15] Radford Ruether comes to the same conclusion: 'The myths of ritual murder, well poisoning and host profanation arose in the wake of crusader violence to provide an image of the Jew as an insidious plotter against Christianity and to justify fanaticism.'[16]

These three 'myths' or libels were widely spread about the Jews after the crusades. The 'ritual murder' charge, made more than a hundred times (including two as late as the twentieth century), claimed that Jews killed Christians in order to obtain their blood for religious rituals. The fact that the Jewish religion forbids the drinking of blood was either unknown or deliberately ignored. The first accusation of this kind was made in Norwich, England, shortly after the First Crusade. The story is as follows: on Good Friday 1141, the body of a child was found, apparently murdered. A claim was made that the 'Jews were responsible'. No evidence was given and no action was taken against the Jews. Nevertheless a cult grew up around the 'victim', which brought pilgrims (and material gain) to the area. Soon similar stories were being told in other towns and even further afield on the continent of Europe, one in Blois (France) as early as 1179, and one in Fulda (Germany) in 1235. (Indeed 'Little Hugh' of Chaucer's *Canterbury Tales* was another of these

13 Davies, p. 358b.
14 Flannery, p. 93.
15 Ibid.
16 Radford Ruether, p. 207

so-called 'martyrs'.)[17] In time, these accusations were followed by torture to obtain confessions and burning at the stake for the convicted. Several popes tried to put a stop to these outrages, and in 1247 Pope Innocent IV ordered an investigation into the charge. The conclusion of the investigators was that the ritual murder charge was nothing other than a Christian invention used to persecute Jews. The Pope subsequently published a bull saying that:

> Although the Holy Scriptures enjoin the Jews 'Thou shalt not kill', and forbid them to touch any dead body at Passover, they are wrongly accused of partaking of the heart of a murdered child at the Passover, with the charge that this was prescribed by their laws, since the truth is completely the opposite. Whenever a corpse is found somewhere, it is to the Jews that the murder is wickedly imputed.[18]

As regards host desecration, this libel claimed that Jews stole the sacred host and pierced it with nails to re-enact the crucifixion. (Variations included stepping on the host.) The fact that Jews do not believe in the presence of Christ in the host and do not consider it to have any significance at all was again either ignored or denied. Flannery says of the host desecration accusations: 'This theme too had a busy career ... embroidered with fantastic and miraculous tales ... often including the bleeding of the host ...'[19] The first of these charges was made in Belitz (Germany) in the twelfth century, where all the Jews of the town were burned,[20] while two

17 Flannery, notes, no. 109, p. 322.
18 Dalin, *The Myth of Hitler's Pope*, p. 30.
19 Flannery, p. 99.
20 Ibid.

particularly infamous incidents happened in Rottingen[21] and Deckendorf.[22]

The charge of well poisoning was probably the most devastating libel of all at the time. The claim made was that the Jews, in an attempt to destroy Christendom altogether, were engaged in poisoning the wells of Europe. When the continent was hit by the plague called the 'Black Death', it brought disastrous consequences for them. The plague reached Europe in the autumn of 1347. It lasted no more than three years, but in that short space of time, 'estimates put the overall population loss at about one-third'.[23] We now know that this disastrous plague was carried to Europe by fleas hosted by rats (there were also some airborne varieties), but this information was not available in the fourteenth century as people sought desperately to discover the source of the disaster. They came to the conclusion that it must have been carried through the water system. The charge was made that the Jews were poisoning the wells, and once again the cry went up that 'the Jews are responsible'. Vicious rumours and stories were then accepted as true and these became the justification for more attacks and killings.

21 Ibid., p. 107. One notorious incident concerns the town of Rottingen. Jews were supposed to have desecrated a host there and a nobleman, named Rindfleisch, stirred up the mob to such a point that the entire Jewish community was put to the stake. Then he marched his followers (called 'Jew Slaughterers') through Germany and Austria pillaging, burning and murdering Jews until the Emperor had to step in to stop them. Emperor Albert I fined the cities responsible, but not before a huge number of people had been killed.

22 Ibid., p. 109. An incident in Deckendorf (or Deggendorf) in 1337 was particularly horrific, because the charge was deliberately fabricated in order to relieve the town of its debts. The Jews were accused of host desecration, attacked and killed, and the town council collected their assets. This incident was also followed by more attacks in fifty-one other towns in Bavaria, Austria and Poland.

23 E.L. Skip Knox, *History of Western Civilization*, Boise State University accessed at www.history.boise. state.edu. 2.2.09.

The following is an example of one of the many outrages perpetrated at this time. It was claimed that a Jewish conspiracy, emanating from Toledo, was plotted by a certain Rabbi Peyret, who had headquarters in Savoy in France. This rabbi, the story went, planned to destroy all Christendom by poisoning the sources of the water supply and had already sent emissaries from Savoy to France, Switzerland and Italy for this purpose. The Count of Savoy, on the basis of this story, gave the order that a number of Jews, who lived near Lake Geneva, should be arrested and tortured in order to obtain confessions. One of those who confessed was a certain Agimet of Geneva (20 October 1348). The following is an extract from his confession. It claims to be part of a conversation between himself and Rabbi Peyret. The latter is quoted as saying:

> We have been informed that you are going to Venice to buy silk and other wares. Here I am giving you a little package of half a span in size, which contains some prepared poison and venom in a thin, sewed leather-bag. Distribute it among the wells, cisterns, and springs about Venice and the other places to which you go, in order to poison the people who use the water of the aforesaid wells that will have been poisoned by you, namely, the wells in which the poison will have been placed.[24]

Agimet confessed that he did as he was told in Venice and then went on to other venues to do the same. We know now that this did not happen at all. Yet 200 Jewish towns and

24 Confession taken from the Appendix to Johann S. Schilter's 1698 edition of the chronicle of the Strasbourg historian, Jacob von Konigshofen (1346–1420).

hamlets were attacked and burnt as a result of this investigation and Agimet's 'confession'. Pope Clement VI condemned the widespread violence resulting from such accusations and pointed out that the Jews suffered from the plague like everyone else. He also declared that they were innocent and issued a bull stating that the accusations were false.[25]

Effect of the Crusades on Trade and Usury

Virtually the only acceptable occupation permitted to Jews in the Middle Ages was trading. This too was affected by the crusades. As a consequence of the latter the routes between east and west were opened up again to Christian traders and for that very reason became unsafe for Jews. Competition and resentment at their prowess added to the danger occasioned by their religion. The only option left them was money-lending or usury, a profession not calculated to endear them to the general population. But princes (clerical as well as lay) needed their services and eventually became protectors of those Jews they employed as financiers. Unfortunately, the princes also regarded 'their' Jews as their financial assets and private property. They taxed them highly and frequently they set the rate of interest to be exacted from customers, a fact not usually taken into account when complaints are made about extortion. No doubt there were some greedy and avaricious Jews, as there were greedy and avaricious Christian money-lenders, but the Jews were in the difficult position of being hard-pressed to find the money demanded of them.[26]

The extent of this hatred can be gleaned from Shakespeare's character, Shylock (from *The Merchant of Venice*), an avaricious, cruel and bloodthirsty usurer. Four

25 Dalin, p. 21.
26 James Parkes, *A History of the Jewish People*, Chicago: Quadrangle Books, 1962, p. 74.

centuries later, this caricature was still in the public mind in England when Charles Dickens created the character of Fagin. It was probably this perception also i.e. of the Jews as owners of, and traders in money, that prompted Pope Eugene III to decide that, in spite of the outrages committed against them during the First Crusade, they should finance the Second Crusade. Perhaps this also explains why St Bernard agreed to that. But Bernard himself wrote: 'I will not mention those Christian money-lenders, if they can be called Christian, who, where there are no Jews, act, I grieve to say, in a manner worse than any Jew.'[27]

Clearly all the injustice and persecution emanating from the crusades was not genuinely motivated by religious beliefs, but sadly it is also clear that the teaching on the Jews handed down by the Fathers of the Church had stigmatised them in such a way as to make it easy to scapegoat them and to use that teaching with evil intent.

THE INQUISITION

The Inquisition is usually linked in our minds with Spain and the over-zealous Catholic monarchs of the sixteenth century, but in fact it was first instituted in France in the thirteenth century as part of a campaign to rid Christendom of heresy altogether. Heresy is described in the *Catholic Encyclopedia* as 'a brand of doctrine substantially differing in some aspect from the doctrine taught by the Church'. It was always a cause of concern for Church leaders. Pope Innocent III, who was elected in 1198, was a strong advocate of orthodoxy and he began a concerted effort to eliminate heresy from Christendom. The 'campaign' that followed lasted long after his death and it was this that inspired the setting up of the Inquisition.

27 *Letters of St Bernard*, op. cit.

The story of Innocent and the heresy that most concerned him, Albigensianism, requires our attention first because of its connection with the Jews. The Albigensians owed their origins to 'the Cathars' or 'the Pure' (descendants of the Manicheans of St Augustine's time, who had made their way to Provence in the twelfth century). Their teaching was extreme (at the other end of the spectrum altogether from the Jewish faith), and included the belief that the material world was evil. The 'Perfect' among them were given to great asceticism and, though not all their followers reached the same 'high standard', many of the faithful were impressed by their strict lives, which highlighted the breakdown in the standards of their own clergy. They showed no hostility to the Jews, however, nor did they object to them holding public office. The Jews for their part sympathised with the Albigensians because of the persecution they suffered as well as appreciating the dignity they afforded them.

Pope Innocent was angered by the attitude of local princes, who showed themselves indifferent to the spread of the Albigensian sect and excommunicated the Count of Toulouse for this very reason. He threatened to excommunicate another prince for his unwillingness to oppose their practice of appointing Jews to public office. Innocent held rigidly to the traditional teaching about the Jews, declaring: '... the Jews, against whom the blood of Jesus Christ calls out, although they ought not to be killed ... yet as wanderers must they remain upon the earth, until their countenance be filled with shame and they seek the name of Jesus Christ, the Lord.'[28]

Frustrated by the lack of cooperation from local princes, Innocent sent his legate to France to deal with the situation (1207). The heretics killed the legate and Innocent called for an armed crusade against them. This call was taken up in 1209

28 Quoted by Flannery, p. 102, from Epistola 10:190 in PL 215:1291.

and a crusade was initiated which continued until 1271 (with an interlude from 1215–1225). Little distinction was made between Jews and Albigensians and many Jews died in the massacres and burnings that were part of this crusade.

It was Pope Innocent also who convened the Fourth Lateran Council (1215), the council responsible for one of the most hated decrees ever made against the Jews: 'Jews and Saracens [are to] wear a special dress to enable them to be distinguished from Christians.'[29] The reason apparently was that since Christians must not associate with heretics, it was important that they recognise them. (Lepers and prostitutes were later added to the list.) In France, Jews were required to wear cloth in the shape of a round yellow sphere, suggesting a gold coin to remind Christians of how Judas had sold his Master for money.

The Order of Preachers (Dominicans) played an important part in the campaign against heresy and the Jews came into conflict with them also. The method used by the Friar Preachers to win over the heretics was called a 'Disputatio' or public debate. Learned Jews often became involved in these debates. They had advanced knowledge of the classics from their links with Spain and, of course, expertise in their own scriptures. Frequently this superior knowledge enabled them to outwit their opponents. This combined with their known sympathy for the Albigensians created tension between them and the Dominicans.

Perhaps this tension explains why surprisingly St Thomas Acquinas, the great Dominican thinker, held so firmly to the traditional teaching about the Jews and even expanded on it. In a letter to the Duchess of Brabant he wrote: 'It would be licit according to custom to hold the Jews, because of their crime, in perpetual servitude, and therefore the princes may

29 Jedin, *The History of the Church*, Vol. IV.

regard their possessions as belonging to the State.'[30] (Confiscation of Jewish property had begun shortly after the death of Charlemagne and it continued apace until Jews were ousted from agriculture altogether.)

The Dominicans were also involved in the burning of the Jewish holy books – the Talmud. These books contain commentaries on the Torah (the Law). As already mentioned, they were first written down in the early rabbinic schools of Javneh and Babylon and comprised the tradition of the 'oral Torah'. The Jews turned to them for spiritual comfort and sustenance in their times of persecution. The earlier part of these writings belongs to that period when tension and disputes between Jews and Christians were expressed in mutually offensive and insulting language (we need only recall St John Chrysostom's sermons), and the Talmud contains some of this polemical material.

When a Dominican Brother, a convert from Judaism, approached Pope Gregory IX with the claim that the Talmud was not only offensive to Christians, but also the cause of Jewish unbelief, the Pope ordered that his claim be investigated. The result of the investigation was that the Talmud was condemned and twenty-four cartloads of copies burned publicly in Paris. After a protest by some rabbis, a second investigation was carried out by St Albert the Great. This also resulted in a condemnation (1248). Subsequently the term 'Talmud Jew' became an insult to throw at the Jews and controversy about the Talmud recurred time and again, in France, Spain and Germany, for centuries to come.

The Tribunal called 'the Inquisition'

Pope Innocent III died in 1216, but the campaign against heresy continued, and in 1233 Pope Gregory IX set up the

30 Flannery, from 'Letter to Duchess of Brabant' (*De Regimine Principum*), Turin: Marietti, 1924, p. 117.

tribunal called the Inquisition. The function of this tribunal was to identify heretics and to sentence those who refused to retract their false teachings. Convicted heretics were not punished by the tribunal but were handed over to the civil authorities for punishment. This treatment of objectors is incomprehensible to us in our day, and even more so when we discover that to obtain confessions, the use of torture was sanctioned (by Pope Innocent IV in 1252). The thinking behind this practice (at that time) is explained in the *New Catholic Encyclopedia* as follows:

> Those who wrote in defense of the use of torture saw the right of immunity as yielding before the greater right of the state to discover quality secrets that menaced its welfare or existence. If the state were not empowered to use torture to get the truth, greater harm would result than would come from violating the liberty of persons or individuals ... No attack of note upon the theoretical basis of the practice was made until the sixteenth century, when various influences, notably among others, the worsening of penal laws under absolutist governments of the time and the extravagances of the witch hunts and trials, caused thoughtful men to seek a fresh view of the practice ...[31]

(Oddly enough, given the methods used, the expressed intention was first and foremost to convert the heretics, and so Pope Nicholas III asked the superiors of the Dominicans and Franciscans to select qualified preachers who would be able to bring them to the truth of the Gospel (1278). Jews were now encouraged to attend sermons designed to convert

31 *New Catholic Encyclopedia*, 2000.

them! Later, in Spain in the thirteenth century, Germany in the fifteenth century, and Italy in the sixteenth century, such attendance was made compulsory. They were still obligatory for Jews in the Papal States up to the end of the nineteenth century.)

Spain and the Inquisition

Big changes had occurred in Spain by now. The period of peace and prosperity enjoyed after the arrival of King Torik was brought to an abrupt end with the arrival of Almohades, another Muslim and a member of the Seljuk family (eleventh century). Almohades was an extreme Islamist and lost no time before decreeing that all his subjects (Christians as well as Jews) must 'Accept Islam or die'. Rather than comply with this decree, Jews and Christians alike fled to the northern kingdoms. At first Jews were accepted there along with their Christian fellows and engaged in all manner of occupation with them. Some of these distinguished themselves in the intellectual, commercial, medical and other fields and princes and kings were happy to bestow positions of power and privilege on them.

However the effort to recover control of the peninsula was soon resumed, and by 1246 was so successful that Granada alone was left under Muslim rule. But this meant that the Iberian peninsula had become a Catholic country with a Jewish minority, a situation that did not augur well for the Jews, and indeed their conditions soon began to deteriorate.

Prior to the conquest by the Muslim, Torik (711), as the reader will remember, Jews were severely persecuted by the Catholic kings, and at the time of that conquest, rumours were circulated that it was they who had invited this attack on the country. Suspicions arising from these rumours were still there in the thirteenth century. The fact that Jews had prospered under Muslim rule itself presented a theological problem for Church authorities. They saw this as being in conflict with the 'servant status' to which Jews were condemned (teaching of St Augustine and his successors).

If this wasn't enough, some of those who had become rich were accused of ostentation. Resentment was growing. Flannery writes: 'Even Jewish chroniclers of these years deplored the manner in which these favoured Jews lived, flaunting their silks and satins, boasting of their lineage, caring nothing for their own people, and devoting little time to their religion or to scholarly pursuits.'[32] The result was that kings and local councils ('cortes') began to apply the anti-Jewish laws of Innocent III and the Lateran Council, and to cancel debts owed to Jews. Jews were excluded from positions involving authority over the baptised, and other restrictions were also imposed. Nevertheless, the laws were not yet as severe in Spain as they were in the rest of Europe.

But resentment continued to grow and in the fourteenth century a series of anti-Semitic sermons, by Peter Olligen a Franciscan, and later, by Ferdinand Martinez, Archdeacon of Seville (1378), were so inflammatory that they resulted in violent physical attacks being made on Jews:

> The death of the king in 1390 gave Martinez the chance, the following summer, to stir up the mobs to attack the Jewish quarter in Seville. The Jewish quarter was ransacked. Some 4,000 Jews were beaten to death in Seville, many more were sold into Arab slavery and some submitted to baptism. Within two weeks, the Jewish communities in the rest of Andalusia were attacked. The riots spread to Cordoba, where about 2,000 Jews were killed, and then to Toledo. In all about seventy Jewish communities in Castile were devastated. The riots

32 Flannery, p. 131.

then spread to Aragon and to Majorca, but not to Navarre or to Portugal. Tens of thousands of Jews are said to have received baptism at this time.[33]

Martinez was condemned by his own bishop and eventually imprisoned. However the 'disbelief' of the Jews was now seen as an urgent problem and Pope Benedict XIII initiated a major campaign to convert them (1412), appointing the Dominican Vincent Ferrer to head the campaign. Vincent warned against the use of violence and urged that conversions be sought by persuasion. The crowds that followed him, however, were not so disciplined and an atmosphere of pressure and coercion pervaded the campaign. Some synagogues were forcibly converted into churches and thousands of baptisms were recorded.

The Pope was pleased with the outcome and considered the campaign to have been a great success. However the circumstances in which these baptisms took place raise questions and problems soon began to arise relating to these new 'conversos'. 'Judaising', or the practice of engaging in Jewish customs and festivals, was perceived to be common and this became an issue. Such practices seemed to others to indicate that the new 'conversos' were reluctant converts at best and that, possibly, they even regretted the step they had taken and had returned to their old faith. It is a matter of record that the 'New Christians' received little or no instruction in their new faith.

There was another problem too: apart from the issue of whether force was used or not, there had also been serious social pressure on the Jews to change their religion since 'conversion' guaranteed them rights that were denied to them as Jews. It would be surprising indeed if some (many were well

33 Peter Hocken, *The Marranos*, TJCII Booklet Series, No. 3, 2006, p. 13.

qualified professional people) were not influenced by mixed motives when accepting baptism. But when 'New Christians' were given important roles in the government, the army, universities etc., the anger and resentment of the 'Old Christians' knew no bounds. They claimed that the converts were false Christians and came to hate them even more than those Jews who had refused baptism altogether. They applied the term 'Marranos' to them, a term that some say translates as 'swine', but was certainly derogatory.

In 1449 riots specifically directed against the 'New Christians' broke out in Castile: 'The rioters in Toledo (capital of Castile) turned on the rich merchants and acquired control of the city.'[34] In response, the local town council passed a law excluding all 'New Christians' from public office in the city. This law, in effect, involved a 'purity of blood' qualification, since it made a distinction between Christians on the basis of their racial origin. People began to say that Jews were intrinsically evil and that Jewish blood itself was the problem. The term 'mala sangre' or 'bad blood' was used and the claim was made that not even baptism could provide a remedy. The horrendous concept of ethnic impurity was born. It was so strongly held that some religious Orders did not accept candidates of Jewish ancestry for a long time to come. (The ban was not removed in the Society of Jesus until the twentieth century.)

In 1460 a collection of the old libel stories, under the name 'Fortress of the Faith,' was published by Alfonso De Spina (a Franciscan). These stories became very popular and an almost feverish Judeophobia followed. Five hundred years later – in a period of similarly irrational hatred of Jews (1912) – the *Catholic Encyclopedia* gave this version of the story:

34 Ibid., p. 14.

At that time the purity of the Catholic faith in Spain was in great danger from the Marranos and the Moriscoes who, for material considerations, became sham converts from Judaism and Mahommedanism to Christianity ... The Marranos committed serious outrages against Christianity and endeavoured to Judaise the whole of Spain.

Given the persecution the Jews were suffering and their relatively small numbers in comparison to Catholics, it would seem more credible to see this as yet another effort by Christians to find an excuse for their actions, in the same way as their forebears had used libel stories to justify the slaughter that took place during the Crusades.

With the marriage of Ferdinand of Aragon and Isabella of Castile in 1479, which united the two remaining Catholic kingdoms in Spain, the persecution became more intense. It seems that the two monarchs were fearful of riots from the start and were persuaded that the real source of the problem was the suspicion raised about the 'New Christians' and their 'Judaising' practices. When de Spina and others called for the introduction of the Inquisition, the new sovereigns consented to seek permission for this from Rome. Pope Sixtus IV granted the permission and he appointed the Dominican, Thomas of Torquemada, as the first Grand Inquisitor in 1483. (The Grand Master was the only appointee of the Pope in Spain, unlike France; all other officials were appointed by the King.)

In theory, the Inquisition was concerned with all offences against the Catholic faith, but from the 1480s until about 1530 in Spain its function was to deal with what Ferdinand and Isabella described as the 'Judaising heresy'. Recent studies suggest that political propaganda opposed to Spanish power at that time exaggerated the activities of the Inquisition in

Spain. However, nobody denies that it did happen and that many Jews were burned at the stake.[35] Sixtus IV, Innocent VIII and Alexander VI intervened to moderate the severity of the early Spanish Inquisition but it seems that they were powerless, as were the Spanish bishops, and that the Inquisition became a law unto itself. Even Thomas of Torquemada, regarded in the past as the greatest villain of all, is said to have checked the excessive zeal of other Inquisitors.[36] However, the *New Catholic Encylopedia* also says of him that: '... he probably encouraged the monarchs to attack both the Marranos and those crypto Jews who had been insincerely or forcibly converted to Christianity and who continued to practice Judaism in secret.'[37]

He seems to have been obsessed by the view that genuine Jews were facilitating the 'Marranos' and he gave orders to the Rabbis (and to the Christians) that they must report such suspects. Not satisfied with the results of these efforts in the end he appealed to Ferdinand and Isabella to have all Jews expelled from the country. The *New Catholic Encyclopedia* continues: 'Exceptionally intolerant even for his time, Torquemada publicised an alleged ritual murder charge in La Guardia to encourage their expulsion ... He tried more suspects than any of his successors.' Ferdinand and Isabella published the decree on 2 January 1492 declaring: 'All Jews must leave the realm on pain of death.'

The long and proud history of the Jews in Spain was at an end. Some of those expelled from Spain found a welcome in Italy or in the Papal States. The Sultan of Turkey also issued an invitation to them. Most, however, preferred to move to Portugal where there had been no previous history of persecution. Alas, times were changing there too.

35 Edward O'Brien, 'A New Look at the Spanish Inquisition', *The Wanderer*, 15 February 1996, p. 201.
36 Ibid.
37 p. 205.

In Portugal King John II removed 700 children from their Jewish families, sending them to an island off the coast of West Africa to be raised as Christians. His successor King Manuel I, hoping to marry the daughter of the Spanish monarchs, realised that if he were to achieve this goal he could not appear to tolerate Jews in his kingdom. Therefore in December 1496 he too issued a decree of expulsion. However, as he did not really wish to lose these new subjects who were a valuable asset to the economy of his country, he arranged that all should be baptised with or without their consent. A Jewish historian writes: 'In Portugal ... the entire Jewish community, both native and immigrant, was dragged to the baptismal font in 1497 and declared to be Christian. The Portuguese Marranos were thus converted as a community.'[38] These 'New Christians' had withstood all temptation to convert in Spain and were stronger in their attachment to Jewish ways than their Spanish counterparts. Virtually none of them believed in Jesus Christ. For a time they were able to live a double life, outwardly Catholic and secretly Jewish, but with the accession of King John III a more repressive regime ensued. In 1536 he instituted the Inquisition.

With Portugal being a much smaller country than Spain, the Inquisition did not have the same difficulties of communication and so was both more effective and more severe there. Many Marranos emigrated. The first to leave went to the Netherlands and later, when Brazil was claimed for Portugal (1500), many fled there also. But the Inquisition followed them even to the New World. With one brief period of interruption, persecution persisted in Portugal until the late eighteenth century.

The Jews were expelled from Spain the same year that Columbus sailed to the New World (1492). So it is not surprising then that we find that by 1600 there were 500

38 Hocken, *The Marranos*, p. 20.

Marranos in Argentina, with others having arrived in Peru, Colombia and Venezuela. It is probable that more than half of the Spanish colonists in Mexico were Marranos. But because of the activities of the Inquisition, they had great difficulty maintaining their Jewish customs. It was too dangerous to keep Jewish books or emblems, and so the task of keeping their traditions alive was carried on, in many cases, by mothers. Descendants of these emigrants today are seeking to recover their lost identity and their Jewish roots. In *Communique of TJC II 2006*, Liliana Saez from Buenos Aires writes of how she discovered through the Internet that: 'Both family names from my mother's and from my father's side were in the lists of Jewish people who had escaped from the Inquisition in Spain.' Liliana goes on to say that, some time later, as she prayed at Plaza 1 de Mayo (site of the first non-Catholic cemetery in Argentina), she experienced

> [A]n internal revolution and a deep pain as I felt in my own soul the horror, the loneliness, the contempt, and the emptiness of knowing that we had been excluded from the Jewish culture and also from the Gentile. Then our identity was lost and we were nearly nothing. ... Who is going to make restitution to us, the Sephardic Jews dispersed in the nations? Jewish parents forced their children to keep silent, Gentiles forced us to keep silent, but 'For the love of Zion, I will not keep silent' (Isaiah 62:1).[39]

The Working of the Inquisition

In fifteenth-century Spain, the difficulty of communication limited the activities of the Inquisitors, yet records show that the work they did was carried out with great efficiency and

39 Liliana Saez, 'TJCII Communique 2006'.

thoroughness. The process itself involved first the gathering of accusations, then confirmations of same, followed up by arrests.

Those arrested were imprisoned in dungeons specially constructed to facilitate spying, and isolation was imposed to add to the pressure to confess. The accused were required (a) to make a confession of guilt, (b) to express repentance, and (c) to request pardon. They were also required to furnish the names of any accomplices or other known Judaisers. The use of anonymous informants and the confiscation of the property of the condemned (up until 1561) led to many false accusations, and torture was frequently used. Those who confessed to a grave offence and repented were obliged to wear a long yellow robe to mark them out. There was no absolution for a second conviction, which led automatically to the stake. The guilty were strangled and their corpses burnt, while the impenitent were burned alive. Initially, sentences were read out at a religious ceremony in church, called an 'auto da fe' (an act of faith.) Later these events became elaborate public spectacles.

It is believed that between 2,000 and 2,500 Marranos, or crypto-Jews, were burned at the stake in Spain, and a total of 1,175 in Portugal.[40] The Inquisition was not confined to France, Spain and Portugal. Pope Eugene IV, under the influence of some Spanish bishops, reversed the policy of his predecessor Martin V when he appointed the Franciscan John Capistrano Inquisitor for the Germanic and Slavonic countries. (John was an over-zealous reformer who had been restrained by Pope Martin V when his preaching in Siena gave rise to attacks on Jews. He was known as 'the Scourge of the Jews'.) However, by this time central Europe was in process of being denuded of Jews altogether. The practice of cancelling

40 Hocken, p. 20.

debts due to them was growing and they were becoming impoverished as a result. They were no longer useful as economic resources and so were expelled from most of the remaining cities in Germany. Therefore the focus of the Inquisition in central Europe was not on the Jews.

The teaching of the Fathers of the Church on the subject of the Jews was accepted in the Middle Ages, with few exceptions. In line with this teaching, ill-treatment of Jews by princes and others was often ignored and sometimes even condoned. The bestowal of honours or privileges on them was strongly objected to by Church authorities. On the other hand, violence against them was denounced by popes and others, but the contradiction between the 'teaching of contempt' and the calls for peace was not addressed.

In the early Middle Ages more benign views about Jews were expressed e.g. by Abbot Rupert of Deutz and St Hildegard of Bingen. Both of these held the view that 'the Jew was the older brother to whom the Father was still offering the ring of faith'. But such views were listened to less and less. 'The farther we get from the early Middle Ages, the more inconsiderate, contemptuous and ironical becomes the tone of the discussion.'[41] The belief that the Church had replaced the Synagogue and the latter was now rejected by God was firmly held. This message was promoted in images of Esau (the older rejected brother) serving the younger Jacob, and of Leah (the older, partially-sighted sister) replaced by the younger and more beautiful Rachel, which decorated churches and chapels all over Christendom. The strong focus of Innocent III and his successors on the elimination of heresy added greatly to the heavy burdens already placed on the children of Israel.

41 *History of the Church*, Vol. IV, New York: Crossroad Publishing, 1982.

CHAPTER THREE

The Ghettos — Italy, Poland, Russia

> The status of the Jews in this era was greatly reduced. No longer hated and feared as a grave peril to Christian society, they were made into objects of aversion and derision. This age which stripped them of all self-respect was, Levinger believes, the 'lowest point in their long and tragic history'.[1]

As we move into the period sometimes called the Modern Age, we find that the Jews have been expelled from England, France, Spain and Portugal, but can still be found living in Italy, the Papal States, and some cities in Germany. Elsewhere survivors of previous persecutions have moved back, either to 'the Land', now called Syria Palestina, or to Poland, the Balkans, or the British Isles.

The threat from the East had risen again when the city of Constantinople was taken in 1453, and Muslim armies had harried the borders of Europe since then. The Jews were suspected of colluding with the Muslims (probably because they had been offered a welcome by the Sultan when they were expelled from Spain), and they were to pay a price for that later. But trouble came first from a different and unexpected quarter.

1 Flannery, p. 149.

The Reformation

Martin Luther's Protest was initiated in 1517. In the beginning, he expected that he would attract conversions to his cause from the Jews and so he espoused their cause in a pamphlet called 'Jesus was born a Jew':

> They [the Papists] have dealt with the Jews as if they were dogs rather than human beings ... If the Apostles, who were also Jews, had dealt with the Gentiles as we Gentiles deal with the Jews, there would never have been a Christian among the Gentiles ... we in our turn ought to treat the Jews in a brotherly manner in order that we might convert some of them ... we are but Gentiles, while the Jews are the lineage of Christ. We are aliens and in-laws; they are blood relatives, cousins and brothers of Our Lord.[2]

The Jews were not, in fact, willing to join the ranks of the 'Protesters' and Luther's message changed: 'Jews are poisoners, ritual murderers, usurers ... Their synagogues should be destroyed ...'[3] His subsequent tracts were so anti-Semitic as to provoke violent attacks on the Jews in Frankfurt-on-Main and also in Worms.

Italy (1550–1870)

All through the Middle Ages Jews and Christians plied their trade almost without disturbance in Italy. They also mingled freely and even inter-married. The tradition of Papal protection was so strong that their 'representatives

---

2   'That Christ was born a Jew' from Walther I. Brandt (ed.), *Luther's Works*, Philadelphia: Muhlenberg Press, 1962, pp. 200–1.
3   Ibid., p. 152, pamphlet, 'Concerning Jews and their Lies'.

participated in the municipal procession on the occasion of the papal coronation, welcoming the new Pontiff, and presenting him with the Scroll of the Law, and accepting a renewal of their rights and privileges'.[4]

In 1550 Cardinal Caraffa was elected pope and took the name Paul IV. Cardinal Caraffa had a history of severity towards Jews and had on one occasion permitted sixty Marranos to be condemned to death by burning. Europe was in the throes of the struggle between the 'Protesters' and the Church and the new Pope seems to have blamed this crisis on the Jews. His immediate predecessors (including the notorious Borgia Pope, Clement VI and the warrior Pope Julius II) had been friendly towards the Jews and had extended privileges to them.

In 1555 Pope Paul IV introduced legislation against the Jews in Rome, in a bull entitled 'Cum nimis absurdum'. The new laws included the wearing of a badge, restriction of work, and housing in what came to be called 'the ghetto': the separate accommodation of Jews from the Christian community under the custody of a Christian guard (for whose services these Jews must pay).[5]

The Jewish quarter in Venice was next to an iron foundry, or 'getto'. The term 'getto' originally referred to the practice whereby Jews were locked away and cut off from the outside world. Most of the cities of Europe that still retained Jewish communities adopted this practice also. These ghettos were usually situated in the poorer areas of large cities and were also usually overcrowded. There was no protection in them from plagues or fires, and disasters of this kind broke out from time to time. (The Roman ghetto, for example, housed 10,000 people in less than two square kilometers and the ghetto in Frankfurt consisted of only one street of 190 houses,

4   Flannery, p. 123
5   Ibid., p. 155, quoted from *Magnum Bullarium Romanum*.

for a population of 4,000.) Jews had lived apart from other communities in the past, and in Christian times the Church encouraged this practice. The Council of Basle (1413) even made it obligatory, but never before had they been locked away in a manner so degrading. The historian Cecil Roth makes this assessment of the effects of the ghetto:

> The circle of human interests was intolerably confined. Life became indescribably petty. There was a superlative degree of inbreeding, physical, social, and intellectual ... By the time that the ghetto had been in existence for a couple of centuries, it was possible to see the result. Physically, the type of Jew had degenerated. He had lost inches off his stature; he had acquired a perpetual stoop; he had become timorous and in many cases neurotic. Degrading occupations, originally imposed by law – such as money-lending and dealing in old clothes – became a second nature, hard to throw off ...[6]

Another historian, Lee Levinger, called it 'the lowest point of their long and tragic history'.[7] In his opinion, Jewish scholarship came to reflect the narrowness of this environment. But, as in other dark periods of their history, the Jewish people turned their focus more than ever to the synagogue and the study of the Torah, and these ghettos became important centres of study where 'the aristocracy of learning' was greatly prized. Looking at it from this perspective, Rabbi Abraham Heschel could say of this time that it was 'a

6   Cecil Roth, *A Short History of the Jewish People*, Oxford: East and West, 1935, pp. 308–9.
7   Flannery, quoted from *Anti-Semitism Yesterday and Tomorrow* by Lee Levinger (New York: Macmillan, 1936, p. 8), p. 149.

golden period of Jewish history, of the Jewish soul'.[8] This was especially true of the Jews of his own native Poland.

Poland (1264–1773)

For many centuries now the Jews had held a particular status in Poland. Back in 1264, when the country was poor and sparsely populated, King Boreslaw invited them to come and help build up his kingdom. He conferred on them their own Charter of Rights. In time, the contribution they made was greatly appreciated and King Casimir the Great (d.1370) conferred on them the unusual privilege of self-government.

This practice, however, was not in accord with the Catholic teaching of the 'servant status of Jews' and Church authorities were unhappy with the situation. The Archbishop of Cracow therefore invited John Capistrano, Inquisitor for Germany and the Slav countries, to come to Poland to deal with it. Capistrano was that fiery fanatical reformer who had acquired for himself the name 'Scourge of the Jews'. He was happy to take on this assignment and he prevailed upon King Casimir IV (1447–92) to extend the usual legal restrictions to the Jews of Poland. Their position deteriorated after that and in the end the ghetto system was imposed there too.

Dissatisfaction and resentment against the Jews was evident also among the ordinary populace who made repeated charges of ritual murder and host desecration. These were accompanied by the customary horrific penalties such as burning at the stake. So having been rewarded for building up and enriching what had previously been a desolate country, the Jews now found themselves at the bottom rung of society, subject to the same persecution from which their ancestors in the rest of Europe had fled.

8   Ibid., quote from Abraham J. Heschel, *The Earth is the Lord's* (Woodstock, VT: Jewish Lights Publishing, 1995, p. 10), p. 148.

This persecution increased when the peasants of Ukraine rebelled against their nobility in 1648. The Polish nobles were hated by their own people because they maintained their own private armies and were constantly at war with each other. This was a source of never-ending misery for their subjects. The nobles employed Jews as their stewards and these stewards lived on the outer rims of their noble's estates. Therefore they became the first targets of the rebellion.

The Swedes were Poland's closest neighbours on the other side of the Baltic Sea, and were referred to at that time as 'the terror of the north'. Taking advantage of the Polish crisis they decided to invade that country and the invasion that followed was so brutal that it is known in Polish history as 'the Swedish Deluge'. The Swedes also picked the Jews out as targets. When the war was over, the Poles accused their Jewish countrymen of collaborating with the enemy and they turned on them as well. These wars were secular and were politically motivated. The Jews, having been associated with the hated nobility, were therefore obvious targets. However the enmity against them cannot be explained by that alone. The Swedes were Lutherans and as such were strongly opposed to the Jews. The Ukrainians were also traditionally anti-Semitic. Moreover they were the people most affected by the supposed collusion with the Muslims. The religious animosity of the Poles has already been demonstrated.

When the carnage of battle was over, persecution persisted in the form of repeated charges of ritual murder and host desecration, which became almost annual events. In their great despair, the Jews appealed to Pope Benedict XIV for help (1758). Benedict responded by appointing Cardinal Ganganelli, a Franciscan, to investigate their complaints. Ganganelli carried out a thorough year-long investigation and concluded that there was a complete lack of evidence for the charges. (Cardinal Ganganelli later became Pope Clement XIV. Rabbi David Dalin says of him: '... from the perspective of the Jews, he was one of history's best popes.')[9]

Despite all the persecution, Jewish education and Talmudic studies advanced so much in Poland at this time that the learning of Polish Jews was renowned and came to have a significant influence on Judaism in general for years to come. It was during this period of intense suffering too that the Hasidic movement was born, a movement that brought joy back into the observance of Judaism and provided a spirituality which lent support to the people in their pain. Its exclusive focus on the Torah and its intolerance of secular study, however, became a source of controversy and division for Jews of later generations.

Russia (1773–c.1920)

The kingdom of Poland-Lithuania enjoyed a golden age in the sixteenth century, but, situated as it was between some of the greatest powers in Europe, it occupied a vulnerable position geographically. After the rebellion and wars of the seventeenth century this vulnerability proved to be disastrous. In fact the kingdom never recovered, and in 1773 the three major powers of Russia, Prussia and Austria began a process of carving up the entire country between them in the 'partitions of Poland'. Overnight the Jews became the subjects of a power that had refused them legal entry into their country since the very beginning of the Christian era. Despised and persecuted in Poland, these very same Jews were now the citizens of a country that, if anything, hated them even more.

Catherine the Great was their new sovereign and it seems that she shared the same feelings as one of her predecessors,

9   Dalin, p. 33.

the Empress Elizabeth, who when asked to accept Jews into the country for commercial reasons, responded with the words: 'From the enemies of Christ I accept no profit.'[10] Catherine exhibited a deep prejudice against the Jewish people from the beginning: she confined them to an area which she called the Pale, taxed them heavily and placed all kinds of legal restrictions on them. Though Catherine pursued a foreign policy that favoured moving closer to the West and passed legislation inviting foreigners into central Russia, she expressly added the phrase 'except the Jews' to the decree.

The fall of Napoleon in 1814 was followed in Russia, as in other countries, by a reaction against the Jews, and severe legislation was introduced against them again. With just a short reprieve under the reign of Alexander I, this situation continued, until the early nineteenth century. The assassination of Czar Alexander II in 1881 then provoked a more intense and vicious persecution. This persecution lasted, with a few short exceptions, right up to the Holocaust and after.

The Pogroms

Russia had a long tradition of revolution and in the past it was convenient for government authorities in such circumstances to divert attention from the harsh rule of the Czars by using 'the Jews' as scapegoats. The assassination of Alexander II created more fear than ever because a new element, nihilism (opposition to all forms of government), had entered into the revolutionary movement and violence was openly advocated as the way to achieve one's goals. Some Jews joined Liberal and Radical movements in the hope of bringing about improvements in their conditions. It is unlikely that they were

10 Flannery, p. 171.

involved in the assassination, but it was inevitable that they would be blamed. An order was promulgated soon after the incident declaring: 'Jews must face death, go into exile or convert to Christianity.'

A spate of pogroms followed this decree. Davies writes: 'In 1881 the town of Yelizaretrad in Ukraine was the scene of an organised pogrom. It was the opening outrage in a wave of attacks over the next three years against the Jewish communities of Kiev, Odessa, Warsaw and Nizhni Novgorod.'[11] One hundred Jewish communities were attacked. Large numbers were maimed, murdered and impoverished, as police turned a blind eye. It seems that the peasants believed they were obeying the will of the Czar. Nothing was done to inform them that this was not so.

Jews fled the country en masse. That year, and every succeeding year in the reign of Alexander III (1881–94), saw one hundred thousand of them emigrate. In 1882 the government had to intervene and put a stop to the pogroms. However, as if to clarify that it was not their intention to exonerate the Jews, they also instituted additional laws against them. The numbers of those emigrating continued to increase and by 1900 one million Jews had left Russia. The international community became concerned and the governments of Britain and the US protested, but the pogroms and oppression continued.

As the revolutionary movement grew in strength, anti-Jewish feeling grew with it. Supporters of the Czar and his regime were convinced that the Jews were (at least in part), responsible for this opposition. The idea that the Jews and the Jews alone were dissatisfied with the harsh rule of the Czars was promoted. A government official named Plehve promised to 'drown the revolution in Jewish blood'. His

11 Davies, p. 844.

statement was followed by the infamous pogrom in Kishinev (1903), which was carefully planned and organised, particularly barbarous, and lasted three days.[12]

More international protests followed, but the Russian authorities were more afraid of revolution within the country than of international opinion. They instituted an organisation called the 'League of Russian People' or 'the Black One Hundreds' in 1904, with the express purpose of combating the 'constitutionalists [those who wanted a representative parliament] and the Jews'. This organisation carried out acts of arson and pogroms openly, with the blessing of the Czar, Nicholas II. So many Jews were killed, wounded, or left homeless that in 1905 the Duma (the Russian parliament) intervened and condemned the pogroms. Their action only served to reveal their powerlessness. In response the government dissolved the Duma. Once again the US protested and even cancelled a trade pact that was about to be made. The British government also protested and cancelled an intended trip by Sir Herbert Samuel (a Jewish Liberal Party MP). Emigration continued. By 1920 three million Russian Jews had reached the US.

International opinion was now beginning to make itself felt and the government needed some 'justification' for its continuing persecution. In 1905 the government press published a book entitled *The Protocols of the Elders*. It proved to be one of the most damaging and lasting libels ever to afflict the Jewish people. The 'inspiration' for this book came from 'Jacob Brafman', a Russian Jew who had converted to Christianity in 1867. 'Brafman', it appears, claimed that the Jews had a world-wide conspiracy aimed at exploiting the Gentile world. From this story came the idea for a book that, it was claimed, contained Jewish documents dating back to 909 BC. These documents allegedly consisted of extracts from

12 Flannery, p. 191.

the work of a Jewish mystic and were supposed to contain plans for a world conquest, the techniques necessary to achieve this, and subsequent steps towards the establishment of a Jewish state.

This book did not become really popular until it was translated into German in about 1919. In 1921 it was exposed as a forgery. (A correspondent with *The Times* in London spotted the close parallel between it and a satire by Maurice Joly on Napoleon III. It was discovered that 50 per cent of the book was taken directly from this work and that the idea for 'the meeting of the elders' came from an adventure story by Hermann Goedsche.) Nevertheless the book enjoyed phenomenal influence as time went on and was translated into numerous languages including German, French, English, Polish, Scandinavian, Italian, Japanese and Arabic. It was popular in England in the 1920s and reached a peak in Germany in the Nazi era. Three editions were published in the US and a Catholic priest, Fr Charles E. Coughlin, ran an anti-Semitic radio programme in the 1930s using it as the source of his propaganda. *The Protocols of the Elders* is still in circulation in the Arab world and Rabbi David Dalin reports that a Lebanese newspaper, *Al-Anwar*, claims that 'a recent edition of the book hit the top of its non-fiction bestseller list'.[13] At the time of its publication, the Russian government claimed that it was used at the World Zionist Congress in Basle in 1897 and this was their excuse for more pogroms and more persecution.

In 1911 a ritual murder charge made against a Jew named Mendel Beilis claimed world-wide attention. A Catholic priest was to be a key witness for the prosecution. Pope Pius X was informed that this priest intended to testify that 'murdering Christian children and drinking their blood is a religious duty

13 Dalin, p. 141.

for Jews' and that the papal documents defending the Jews from ritual murder charges were forgeries. The Pope wrote to Lord Leopold Rothschild (an eminent Jew living in London) verifying the accuracy and authenticity of (1) Pope Innocent IV's bull of protection for the Jews, and (2) of Cardinal Ganganelli's report refuting the blood libel. The Russian Embassy in London forwarded the letter to Beilis's attorneys. This action probably helped to secure his acquittal in 1913, but only after a two-year trial. The Russian government was once again discredited in the eyes of the world.[14]

The Jews and Communism (or Bolshevism)

However, it would be a mistake to think that the 'outside world' was now in complete sympathy with the Jews. On the contrary, despite awareness of the pogroms and protests against them, the common perception was that all Jews were Bolsheviks and were therefore to blame for the rise of Communism. This was 'reason' for persecution of Jews outside of Russia in many countries. The perception itself was false, though one can see the cause for its rise.

Lenin and his followers actually formed only one group in the Russian Social Democratic Party. There were at least two more, both of which were made up of Jews: the Bundists and the Zionists. The Bundists were those who looked for self-determination for all ethnic groups in the Empire, as well as better conditions for their own people. The Zionists were those who would be satisfied with nothing less than a homeland in Palestine. Lenin had little respect for either group and in any case believed that he did not need them, as revolution was best achieved by a small number. The Jewish masses never supported the Red cause. Jewish names did

14 Ibid., p. 35.

appear in the highest ranks of the Soviet government in its beginnings e.g. Trotsky, Radek, Zinoviev, Kamenev. But all of these men had either abandoned faith in Judaism or had never practiced it. (During the reign of the Czars many of the Jewish intelligentsia had had to go abroad to study, and some were influenced by the thinking of Karl Marx.) Marxism has often been referred to as 'Jewish Marxism' since Marx was a Jew by birth, but the reality was that his parents adopted Christianity when he was a child and he was baptised at the age of six and brought up a Christian. Rabbi Isaac Herzog, responding to that accusation made in Ireland, had this observation: 'He [Marx] never had any association with the Jewish community or came under Jewish influence.'[15]

In 1917, the year of the Communist Revolution, the vast majority of Jews in Russia favoured the Mensheviks (liberal socialist opponents of the Bolsheviks), and the worst of all the waves of pogroms against Jews occurred in the year of the Bolshevik Revolution itself. The massacre at Novgorod Severskyi was carried out by the Red (Bolshevik) Army whose war cry was: 'Beat the bourgeoisie and the Jews.' In the end, Lenin outlawed the pogroms and condemned anti-Semitism as counter-revolutionary. His own Red Army was not pleased with this decision and the White Army (representatives of the Church and the Czar) was more antagonised than ever. To add to their problems, the Jews lived in the area of Russia where the battle lines moved back and forth throughout the war (1914–18), and so they were held responsible whenever reverses occurred on either side. The Russian government accused many of them of espionage and deported them to Siberia. In 1918 when the war was over more pogroms followed.

Branded as the enemies of Christ and the Church, the Jews, condemned to live in the misery of the ghettos, were

15 Dermot Keogh, *Jews in Twentieth Century Ireland*, Cork: Cork University Press, 1998, p. 98.

blamed (1) for the Reformation (Italy), (2) for the harshness of the nobility, the threat of the Turks, and the slaughter by the Swedes (Poland), and (3) for Communism and the Revolution (Russia and much of the rest of Europe). Persecution followed those who fled to eastern Europe (seventeenth and eighteenth centuries) and persecution brought many back to the west again (eighteenth and nineteenth centuries). When at last it seemed that civil emancipation and assimilation offered hope for the future, the deep-seated anti-Semitism of Europe once again gained the upper hand and the results were worse than anyone could have anticipated.

CHAPTER FOUR

From the Ghetto to the Birth of Zionism

> I know this people well. It has no spot on its hide which does not ache, where there is not some old bruise, some ancient pain, some secret woe, the memory of a secret woe, a scar, a wound, a laceration of the Occident or of the Orient. They bear their own woes and all the woes of others. Thus every Jew in annexed Alsace and Lorraine was made to suffer as a Frenchman.[1]

The Jews had been absent from most of western Europe for two hundred years, but when they fled back to central Europe from the wars in Poland they found that, despite their long absence, anti-Semitism was alive there still. In Germany the controversy about the Talmud was still in progress, and an account of all the old libel stories against them entitled *Judaism Unmasked* was published in 1700. The Empress Maria Theresa (r.1745–65), who ruled what was now called the Empire of Austria-Hungary, expelled the Jews from Bohemia and only agreed to revoke the decision when persuaded by European sovereigns acting on the pleas of some privileged court Jews. She also enacted humiliating decrees such as: Jews must always walk in twos; Jews must not appear in public

---

1 Quoted from Peguy's 'Cahiers de la Quinzaine' in Raissa Maritain, *We Were Friends Together*, London: Longman Green & Co., 1942, p. 58.

when there is a prince in town; Jews must not be allowed to buy ahead of a Christian at the markets; Jews must be required to have a 'pass' to travel; Jews must pay a body tax in transit.[2]

Most Jews who still remained in that part of the world lived (like their counterparts in Poland) in the deplorable conditions of the ghettos, often having to turn to wealthy fellows court Jews for help to pay these taxes. Then, miraculously almost, out of these ghettos came new hope. Moses Mendelsohn, a Jew who was reared and educated in the environment of the ghetto, broke out of the restrictions of his environment to become a brilliant philosopher. He saw how the closed system of the ghetto was damaging his fellow Jews and looked for ways to help them. In pursuit of this goal he approached Wilhelm Dohm, the Councillor of State in Prussia, with the request that he plead with the Emperor to grant civil emancipation to Jews. Not only did Dohm agree to this request, but he added a statement to his plea which laid the blame for the stagnation and degradation of the Jews on the Christian world.

And so it happened that only one year after the death of Maria Theresa (1780), her successor, the Emperor Joseph II (r.1765–90) issued a Patent of Tolerance which abolished the obligatory badge, the body tax and other restrictions and granted access to schools and universities to Jews. At the same time he obliged Jews to include liberal studies and the German language in their curricula. Mendelsohn and his followers were delighted, but more conservative Jews viewed the inclusion of secular subjects as unacceptable. Young Jews responded by applying to enter the universities in such numbers that other Germans feared they would be over-represented. Many of these young men were anxious to

2   Flannery, p. 154.

assimilate with the society around them (a reaction, perhaps, to years of being cut off) and some were willing to relinquish their faith for this purpose.

Famous names associated with anti-Semitism at this time in Germany included Fichte, Hegel, Stirner and Goethe. That their particular brand of anti-Semitism was nationalist and racist in character bode ill for the future. Hegel enunciated the 'doctrine' of the 'racial inferiority' of the Jews and his follower, Max Stirner, propounded the view that the Jews had never surpassed the 'negro' stage of human evolution, but were primitive, like the Christians, who had 'a slave morality' in contrast to the 'master morality' of the Romans and Teutons.[3]

In France the popular precursors of the Revolution, Voltaire, Rousseau and Diderot, were all anti-Semitic. Though Voltaire professed to be a deist and not a Christian, he still let it be known that he agreed with the massacres and persecutions carried out by Christians on Jews in the past. He was also a personal friend of Frederick II of Prussia, another anti-Semite, and had many discussions with him on the subject, which have been recorded. (It is said that Hitler studied these discussions at the beginning of his career.)[4] Nevertheless it was in France that civil emancipation was first granted to the Jews – though not without a struggle. Illogical though it might seem, Jews were not included in the 'Declaration of the Rights of Man' in 1789. It took two years of their own hard work for them to be finally included.[5]

Napoleon's conquests in Europe brought emancipation to the Jews there (except in Austria and the Papal States) and the

3 Flannery, p. 181.
4 Cited in Flannery, p. 176, from *Hitler's Secret Conversations 1941–1944*, New York: Farrar, 1953.
5 Dan Cohn-Sherbok, *The Crucified Jew – Twenty Centuries of Christian Anti-Semitism*, Grand Rapids, MI: Eerdmans, 1997: also Davies, p. 844.

revolutions of 1848, which resulted in legislative assemblies being set up all around Europe, benefited Jews also as they too were allowed to take their places in them. England, on the other hand, where representative government was an older institution, was slow to respond to this development. For example, though Baron Lionel de Rothschild was elected member for the city of London in 1841, it was not until 1858 that he was permitted to take his seat.[6] As early as 1828, Rabbi Isaac Goldsmid sent to Ireland to enlist Daniel O'Connell's support for a Bill of Parliament to remove Jewish civil disabilities.

By the second half of the nineteenth century then, Jews enjoyed civil equality in most of the countries of western Europe. But it soon became clear that this legal equality did not necessarily mean a change of heart. At first glance the Industrial Revolution and the changes it brought about should have been particularly beneficial to Jews. Old systems and structures were breaking down and there were opportunities for involvement in commercial activity. In the past, when jobs were available and no feudal structures existed, Jews had been able to trade equally with Christians (e.g. in Italy and Ireland). Now, however, newcomers complained that the Jews were entering this world as 'conquerors' and resentment flared once again. Indeed most Jews had been involved in trading of one kind or another before this and were better prepared therefore for the competitive economic environment in which they now found themselves. Moreover many distinguished themselves in the field. This now became the grounds for a new charge claiming that 'Jews are involved in a worldwide financial conspiracy to wield power over Christians'. It was even said that they had seized control of international gold for this purpose.[7] A French writer, Toussenel, produced a book called *The Jews,*

6   Flannery, p. 166.
7   Ibid., p. 167.

Kings of the Epoch, in which he described Jews as 'the people from hell' and denounced them for what he called 'Jewish unproductiveness' and 'parisitism'. (This would become the official position of anti-Semitic Socialists, while those who opposed Socialism denounced it as 'Jewish Marxism'!)

Emancipation, in fact, turned out to be a mixed blessing, especially in France. Since the Revolution of 1789 the entire country was deeply divided. Royalists, representatives of the Church and all who supported the 'ancien régime' hated the Republic and all that it stood for. Church leaders believed that it was essentially anti-clerical and, as in the past, laid the blame for this anti-clericalism, together with the declining influence of the Church, on the Jews. The Republic had granted them 'emancipation' and so its opponents referred to the Republic as 'the Jew Republic'.

Germany

The Catholics in the National Liberal Party were the force behind the granting of civic emancipation to the Jews of Prussia in 1848. (This was not in line with the policy of the Papal States under Pius IX, the reigning Pope.) This party also supported Bismarck in his campaign to unite Bavaria and Prussia and create the German Empire. However, when Bismarck made peace with the Catholic Church (Kulturkampf, 1871), he turned his back on the National Liberals and anti-Semitism reared its ugly head once more.[8]

Bismarck's tacit support for this anti-Semitism enabled him to unite disparate groups and strengthen his own position. When a financial crash in the markets was followed by a literary war (including physical violence) against Jews, and three hundred thousand petitions were signed asking for the reinstatement of the old restrictions against them, he

8   Ibid., p. 180.

responded by limiting the numbers of Jewish entrants into universities. He also held two ritual murder trials. The unrest continued, Jews were insulted in the streets, anti-Jewish boycotts were organised, a synagogue was burned and an anti-Semitic congress was held.

The nationalism that made the unification of Germany possible was fed in part by the racist anti-Semitism already mentioned. To this way of thinking the Jew was by definition 'alien' and there was nothing he or she could do about it. As in Spain of old, Jewish 'blood' was the problem and even baptism itself could not change that. The catch-cry of nationalism, 'Blut und Boden' ('Blood and Soil'), did not include the Jew, and a slogan (invented by a historian named Trietchke) 'The Jews are our misfortune', became popular. Another version of old libels, *The Talmud Jew,* was published by Fr August Rohling (1871) and a book called *The Foundation of the 19th Century* by an Englishman named Chamberlain (who became a naturalised German citizen) promoted the idea of Teutonic superiority and Jewish baseness. Seeds of a dreadful harvest were being sown.

France

Things were not improving in France either. In 1886 Edouard Drumont produced a book called *La France Juive*, which he claimed was a Catholic publication written for the purpose of opposing anti-clericalism. In fact, the book accused the Jews of responsibility for all the woes of France since medieval times. Drumont didn't stop there, but carried out a veritable campaign against them, adding pamphlet after pamphlet which repeated his attacks on the Jews and on the Republic. The anti-Jewish hatred whipped up by this campaign, together with what was already there, was demonstrated most shockingly in the Dreyfus Affair.

Captain Alfred Dreyfus was the only Jew on the general staff of the French army. He was accused of spying for the

Germans, tried secretly, convicted, and imprisoned on Devil's Island (1894). Dreyfus protested his innocence. The only evidence for the accusation against him was an unsigned letter purported to be in his hand-writing. Colonel Picquart, a Catholic, soon became suspicious that the real culprit was a Major Esterhazy, but when he reported this to his superior officer he was told to keep silent and was sent on mission to Tunisia. A year or so later Picquart informed the vice-president of the senate of his suspicions and a publisher named Clemenceau decided to take up the case. An article entitled 'J'Accuse' by Emile Zola was published in the newspaper *L'Aurore* and as a result Zola was tried for libel and convicted. He fled to England, Picquart was arrested, while Esterhazy was tried and acquitted. However, some time later (1898), when Esterhazy had been discharged for dishonesty, he confessed to an English reporter that he had, in fact, forged the letter for which Dreyfus had been condemned.

In order to save the reputation of the army, another officer, Colonel Henry, then forged new documents but he was exposed and committed suicide. The case was re-opened and Dreyfus was given a new sentence of ten years! The President of the Republic intervened at this point and annulled sentence, but to grant a pardon! In 1903, to clear his name, Captain Dreyfus himself requested a revision of the case and at last he was acquitted of all charges in 1906.

The level of anti-Semitism unleashed by this affair was so great that, as Flannery comments, 'for a while no Dreyfusard was safe in all France'.[9] Catholic publications, including *La Croix*, brought this anti-Semitic hatred onto the streets. The hatred of the Jews that had been stirred by the Dreyfus Affair, though abating for a short while, remained just below the surface.

9   Flannery, p. 186.

Theodor Herzl, an Austrian Jew, was, like Mendelsohn before him, deeply concerned about the situation of his people. Having benefited from civil emancipation and assimilated into French society, he participated, as a news correspondent, in the trial of his fellow Jew. Seeing at first hand the injustice endured by Dreyfus, he came to the conclusion that emancipation had not solved the predicament his people found themselves in. He decided then that Jews would never be free of persecution until they possessed their own state and were in control of their own destiny. On this account he presented a paper on the subject, 'Der Judenstat' (the Jewish State) at the World Zionist Congress in Basle in 1897. He wrote in his diary in September of that year: 'At Basle I founded the Jewish State. If I said this aloud today I would be answered by universal laughter. Perhaps in five years, certainly in fifty, everyone will see it.'[10]

The Papal States

We cannot move on into the next century without mentioning the tragic Mortara Affair, which occurred during the reign of Pope Pius IX (elected in 1846 – two years before the 1848 revolutions). Though the new Pope was considered a liberal at the time of his accession, the revolution in Rome had a deep and, it would seem, negative effect on him. Davies says of the effects of the 1848 revolutions: '... the higher echelons of the Catholic hierarchy had been shocked to the roots by the events of the revolutionary era, and were frozen into an ultra-conservative stance from which they did not begin to emerge until the 1960s.'[11] Pope Pius IX shared in this ultra-conservative mindset and, in the opinion of the same historian, made decisions that 'were so extreme that the Papacy lost much respect both within and without the

10 Martin Gilbert, *Israel: A History*, London: Black Swan, 1998, p. 15.
11 Davies, p. 797b.

Church'.[12] Whether this assessment is correct or not, there is no doubt that his decision relating to the Mortara Affair caused scandal both 'within and without the Church'.

The story concerns a Jewish child named Edgardo Mortara who was baptised secretly by a Catholic nurse at the age of seven years without the consent of his parents. She informed a priest of what she had done and, to the despair and helplessness of his parents, the papal gendarmes arrived unexpectedly at their house and removed the boy. The boy was taken to the Pope, who assumed guardianship over him. Despite the parents' repeated pleas that they see their son, they were refused access and did not achieve this until the Papal States were taken over by Victor Emmanuelle II (1870). It was Victor Emmanuelle who in the end gave orders for the meeting to take place. But Edgardo was now a grown man and had become a seminarian. He did not wish to return to his family. We are told that his father returned home 'a broken man'.[13] Edgardo always maintained that he was well treated and cared for by the Pope. He was eventually reconciled with some members of his family.

This decision of Pius IX is beyond comprehension in our time. One can only surmise that the Pope was influenced by some law or other – possibly the decree of a Council of Toledo in the seventh century which stated that: '... force must not be used in baptism, but those who had already received the sacrament must remain Christians and also avoid relations with unbaptised Jews; in cases where the children of unbaptised Jews had been baptised, the children were to be taken from them for Christian education.'[14] Or, perhaps, the teaching of Innocent III in the thirteenth century, that:

12 Davies, p. 797c.
13 David I. Kertzer, *The Kidnapping of Edgardo Mortara*, New York: Picador, 1997, Chapter 25.
14 Flannery, p. 76 (from Code of Canon Law of Benedict XIV, 1740–1758).

'Whoever is led to Christianity by violence, by fear and torture ... receives the imprint of Christianity and can be forced to observe the Christian faith.'[15] The affair was considered so scandalous that it was taken up by nationalists such as Garibaldi and Mazzini, and some historians believe that it was the Pope's handling of this 'affair' that empowered Victor Emmanuel in his actual takeover of the Papal States. Pius IX also has the unpopular reputation of having maintained the ghetto in Rome long after it was abandoned elsewhere, as well as obligatory sermons (for Jews) right up to 1870. But with the entry of Victor Emmanuel into the city the gates of the ghetto were burnt down.

USA

Finally, before concluding this part of the story, we need to note the growing numbers of Jews living by this point in the USA. Back in the 1820s they had been accepted as hard-working members of society, but as their numbers grew, old European caricatures began to emerge. For example, as in similar situations in Europe, when both sides in the American Civil War were perceived to include Jews, this gave rise to the accusation that the Jews as a race were disloyal! The first public act of discrimination against them here occurred in Saratoga in 1877. The Grand Union Hotel refused entry to a Jewish patron and his family. Jews had experienced discrimination before this in the army and in the government, but this was not publicly known. After Saratoga, the practice became open and publicly acceptable and a form of apartheid followed as Jews were excluded from resorts, clubs and private schools.

When a new wave of immigrants arrived from Russia, between 1881 and 1891, and competition for jobs increased,

15 Ibid., p. 136 (from *Regesta Pontificum Romanorum*, 1479).

violence and discrimination increased also. There were reported beatings of Jews in the streets of New York and Boston. People made distinctions between new, so-called 'alien' Jews, and the older stock. The remarkable success of some of the new immigrants was viewed with suspicion, and sinister questions were asked about invisible money powers, gold, and a Jewish oligarchy. Fear was even expressed that this 'oligarchy' would make Christians pay for past persecutions of Jews.

Anti-Semitism continued to thrive even when there were few Jews about and after they had been legally granted civil emancipation. This anti-Semitism was not specifically Catholic or Christian, but, as in France, Italy and Germany, the Church was heavily involved. The economic issue was still a factor too and scapegoating of Jews continued wherever scapegoats were required. But increasingly this ancient anti-Semitism was wedded to a racist and nationalist brand of Jew hatred. The scene was set for the horrors that were about to come.

CHAPTER FIVE

The Holocaust
– Participators and Collaborators

> In this kingdom of darkness there were many
> people. People who came from all the occupied
> lands of Europe. And then there were the Gypsies
> and the Poles and the Czechs ... it is true that not
> all the victims were Jews. But all the Jews were
> victims.[1]

At the turn of the twentieth century intense persecution was
still the lot of the Jews in Russia. Zionists led by Theodor
Herzl began seriously trying to prepare the way for a Jewish
homeland in Palestine. After he had received a refusal from
the Sultan, he approached the British government and was
offered a homeland in Uganda. This was not what Herzl had
in mind, but because of the dire situation in Russia he decided
to accept, on a temporary basis. His decision was received
with anger, especially from the Russian Jews who were
interested in no other homeland except one in 'the Land'
(that of their ancestors). Jews had, in fact, begun to trickle
back there in the 1820s, and in 1878 some of those living in
Jerusalem set up a settlement called 'Gateway of Hope'.

Chaim Weizmann, later first president of Israel, and his
negotiating team won Britain's support for a Jewish homeland

---

1 Elie Wiesel (from quote given on Holocaust Memorial Day, Ireland,
2006).

in Palestine. A number of factors strengthened their hand in this endeavour. The British were hoping to become the dominant power in the Middle East. The family of one of the members of Weizmann's team was already helping them set up a spy ring in Palestine. Weizmann himself, a brilliant young chemist, had at the request of the then Lord of the Admiralty, Winston Churchill, already come to the rescue of the Royal Navy, producing thirty tons of acetone to manufacture cordite gunpowder. The British government for its part was anxious to obtain Jewish support in Russia where the war effort was in danger of being sidelined by the revolution. (Their hope to control the Middle East could hardly materialise in the absence of Russian support.) There was another motive also. Arthur Balfour, the Foreign Secretary, had a personal interest in the 'people of the Book'. He believed that Christians owed 'an immeasurable debt' to the Jews and that restoring them to their homeland was a way of paying some of that debt. As Puritans in the seventeenth century and Evangelicals in the eighteenth century had also advocated the restoration of the Jewish homeland, there was a tradition established in England to support the view that the British public was behind him.

Whatever the deciding factor, Arthur Balfour gave official support for a Jewish homeland in Palestine on 2 November 1917 with the famous declaration named after him:

> His Majesty's government views with favour the establishment in Palestine of a National Home for the Jewish people, and will use their best endeavour to facilitate the achievement of this object ...[2]

Events in the war were favouring the Zionists also. Turkey had allied herself with Germany at the beginning of the war, so

2   Martin Gilbert, *Israel: A History*, New York: Doubleday, 1998, p. 34.

when the British and French armies were unable to break the deadlock on the western front, the British decided to link up with Russia. This meant that they had first to take on the Turkish army. The Turks (unexpectedly) were ready for them and the British troops were roundly defeated at Gallipoli (April 1915). However, when the Turks later expelled the Jews from Jerusalem, British troops under General Allenby proceeded from Egypt, which they already occupied, captured the city and accepted the keys from the Turks on 11 December 1917 – less than a month after Balfour's declaration. If the British were true to their promise, a homeland for the Jews in Palestine was in sight.

World War I came to an end in 1918 and a year later the Peace Treaty was signed at Versailles. The Jewish delegation presented petitions to the conference and almost all of them included a request for the implementation of the Balfour Agreement. The decision on this was at first postponed until the following year at San Remo and on that occasion the British government was given the Mandate of the region. This decision was opposed by the Arabs, who showed their opposition by rioting in the streets of Jerusalem.

Anti-Semitism between the Wars (1918–1939)

Anti-Semitism decreased immediately after World War I but, as inflation increased and the economic situation deteriorated, Jews became the scapegoats once more. Most of European Jewry lived in Poland and Russia but Romania, Hungary and Austria also had sizeable Jewish populations. We now look briefly at relevant developments in those and other countries.

Poland

The Poles were strongly opposed to Bolshevism and associated the Jews with that ideology. This was the motivation behind the many pogroms that occurred there at this time. In fact, so many pogroms were carried out that President Wilson and the Allied Powers decided to intervene. General Pilsudki, who came to power in 1926, had been involved in the war against the Bolsheviks prior to this. He did put an end to the violence but instituted in its place a policy called 'the cold pogrom': impoverishing the Jews, thus leaving many of them destitute. The problem grew when their co-religionists began to arrive as refugees from Germany.

Russia

There was little change in Russia either. Some Jews took advantage of Lenin's New Economic Policy (allowing for competition), but they were later blamed for its implementation and subsequently discriminated against in housing and taxation. Collectivisation affected the Jews more seriously than others because, having never worked the land, those who did not get jobs in the bureaucracy were left with nothing at all. Things improved slightly after Stalin initiated his Five Year Plan (1930). Millions of jobs became available and there was very little overt anti-Semitism in those five years. But with his first purge (1935) many Jews in high positions were 'liquidated', and when Stalin entered into his pact with Hitler (1939) it became the duty of Russian soldiers to help round up Jews for extermination.

Romania

Romania had a history of anti-Semitism and completely ignored the Treaty of Versailles, removing Jewish citizenship rights (guaranteed – on paper – by that Treaty) and blaming the Jews for its deteriorating economic circumstances.

Hungary

The position was aggravated in Hungary by the fact that it was ruled until 1919 by a hated dictator, Bela Kuhn, himself

of Jewish birth. His fall was followed by a general
persecution of the Jews.

Austria

Many young Jews in search of education emigrated to Austria
in the nineteenth century. By the beginning of the twentieth
century many of them had risen to positions of great
prominence. Extraordinary success had been achieved in the
areas of education, music and medicine. Well-known names
such as Freud and Mahler spring to mind but there were many
more besides. Native Austrians were threatened by this, and
they feared that Vienna was being taken over by the Jews.
There was increasing tension in relation to this issue.

France

The extreme nationalism evidenced in the Dreyfus Affair at
the beginning of the century was continued by Maurice
Barres and Charles Maurras, founders of Action Française,
which had as its slogan 'France for the French'. But the advent
of Henri Bergson, the popular Jewish philosopher, resulted
in a shift in favour of Jews. The lay Catholic movement led by
Jacques Maritain, which supported the Jews, also had a
positive influence. In 1936 France elected Léon Blum Prime
Minister, the first Jewish man to hold this position.

England

There was no obvious discrimination against Jews in England
but the *Protocols of the Elders* caused a stir in the 1920s. The two
most prominent Catholic writers, G.K. Chesterton and Hillaire
Belloc, both expressed anti-Semitic views. Chesterton had many
Jewish friends and was unequivocal in his opposition to Hitler
from the start, but he was wont to 'joke' about the supposed
Jewish 'love of money' (which was unfortunate, given the
particular historical slant of English prejudice). Belloc, however,
was strongly prejudiced against them. His book, *The Jews*, is

entirely devoted to what he calls 'the problem of the Jews'. Printed first in 1922, it was reprinted a number of times, the last edition appearing in 1937.[3]

Italy

At the beginning of his career Mussolini supported his country's history of good relations with Jews and even declared that anti-Semitism was 'barbaric'. But all that changed when he joined up with Hitler.

USA

By 1920 there were more than three million Jews in the United States. (There were three million Russian Jews alone.) The atmosphere was one of social and economic rivalry and the fact that some Jews were successful and became rich evoked resentment and discrimination. In 1924 the government moved to restrict the number of Jewish immigrants. Jews were already publicly barred from some professions. Advertisements for jobs began to read 'Gentiles only' or 'Christians only' and large areas of cities and suburbs were closed to anyone of 'Hebrew descent'. Anti-Semitic literature appeared with 'findings' that Jews were pathological and inferior. The lowest point, however, must have been in 1928 when a ritual murder charge was made in New York State and the local police responded by taking the rabbi in for interrogation. This outrageous accusation was, even at this late date and in the so-called civilized New World, taken so seriously that his interrogation continued all through the night. The missing child re-appeared at dawn, explaining that she went into hiding when she realised that she was lost.

Anti-Semitism increased in the States with the Depression, as it did everywhere else. Jews were 'last to be hired and first to be fired'. One hundred and twenty-one anti-Semitic

3   London: Longman & Co.

organisations emerged between 1937 and 1939, while William Pillay and Louis McFadden ran for the presidency on anti-Semitic tickets. As already mentioned, Fr Charles E. Coughlin ran an anti-Semitic radio station using the *Protocols of the Elders* as source for his propaganda. The number of his listeners reached three and a half million. But he was removed from his post after the visit of Cardinal Pacelli (later Pope Pius XII) in 1936. The Cardinal had a private meeting with President Roosevelt on this occasion and Rabbi David Dalin reports, 'most important to American Jews ... was his behind-the-scenes role in silencing the notorious anti-Semitic radio priest'.[4] It appears that President Roosevelt had expressed his concerns to the Cardinal about Coughlin's propaganda. At the beginning of the war, some Americans complained that the Jews were forcing their country into it, but as time went on these feelings changed and anti-Semitism abated.

Germany

However we must give our principal attention to Germany here since she was the main player in the Holocaust. The extreme nationalism referred to earlier, expressed in the phrase 'Blut und Boden', had taken root, and the so-called 'alien' Jew had become the scapegoat for all the problems of the nation. Claims were made that the Jews had both caused and lost World War I. Not only that but they were said to have 'shirked' their responsibility on that occasion, despite the fact that 100,000 Jews (out of a population of 565,000) had served in the war, 80 per cent of them on the front line. Disillusionment and resentment at the repayments imposed by the Conference of Versailles were the cause of increasing anger among the young and unemployed.

4   *The Myth of Hitler's Pope*, p. 58.

Sebastian Haffner was a young 'Aryan' who escaped Germany just before the outbreak of World War II. Later he became a journalist and gave an account of his personal experience of the Nazi era in a book entitled *Defying Hitler*. Haffner tells of how, as an eleven year old, he and his friends studied the daily bulletins describing the progress of World War I from the beginning. He recounts how day after day they read the glorious reports of German victory and then, to utter disbelief and devastation, the final bulletin of defeat:

> The terms [of the armistice] no longer spoke the careful language of the army bulletins. They spoke the merciless language of defeat – as merciless as the bulletins had been when they spoke of enemy defeats. The fact that such a thing could happen to 'us', not as an isolated incident, but as the final result of victory upon victory, just would not fit in my head ... I read the terms again and again, craning my neck, as I had done for the last four years. At length I withdrew from the crowd and wandered off, not knowing where ...[5]

This extreme disillusionment pervaded the whole country. The fact that Germany had been defeated was incomprehensible to its people and, as unemployment, inflation and a worsening economy followed, there was widespread unrest. In retrospect we can see that the country was ripe for a demagogue such as Hitler. Everyone, especially the young, was clutching for some straw. This made it easy for Hitler to whip up mob support by providing a simple, however false, solution: 'The Jew is the cause of every problem, the destroyer, the poisoner of Aryan blood ... the epitome of evil ... inherently and uneradically ... neither baptism nor the

5   Blaine, WA: Phoenix, 2003, p. 23.

renunciation of Judaism could redeem him.' The obvious solution therefore was 'Jewry Perish'. (Referring to his anti-Semitism at a later stage Hitler would note it '[b]eyond doubt the most important weapon in my propaganda arsenal'.)[6]

The Nazi Party expressed its goals in these simple terms: (1) to organise the rebirth of the German nation; and (2) to oppose the Jews. And so when Hitler became chancellor in 1933, the period of terror for the Jewish people began. On 1 April of that year, newspapers announced that all Jewish shops, doctors, and lawyers must be boycotted; shops both 'Aryan' and Jewish must sack their Jewish employees; and Jewish owners of businesses must withdraw from their businesses and install 'Aryan' managers in their place. Haffner gives this account:

> That year the Nazis no longer felt any restraint. With their gangs they regularly broke up the election meetings of other parties. They shot one or two opponents every day ... The new Prussian regional interior minister (a Nazi: a certain Captain Göring), promulgated an incredible decree. It ordered police to intervene in any brawl on the side of the Nazis, without investigating the rights or wrongs of the matter, and furthermore to shoot at the other side without prior warning.[7]

The same writer also tells of how an 'education' campaign was set up so that Germans could learn that 'it had been a mistake to consider the Jews as human beings ... In reality they were a kind of "subhuman" animal, with the characteristics of a devil'. As a young man who numbered Jews among his close friends, Haffner was very affected by what happened next:

6   Flannery, p. 210.
7   *Defying Hitler*, p. 91.

> Apart from the terror, the unsettling and depressing aspect of this first murderous declaration of intent was that it triggered off a flood of argument and discussions all over Germany, not about anti-Semitism but about 'the Jewish question' ... Suddenly everyone felt justified, and indeed required, to have an opinion about the Jews, and to state it publicly ... The defenders of the Jews were frowningly told that it was reprehensible of the Jews to have such and such a percentage of doctors, lawyers, journalists etc. Indeed percentage calculations were a popular ingredient of 'the Jewish question'. People discussed whether the percentage of Jews among the Communist Party was not too high, and among the casualties of the Great War, perhaps too low.[8]

The year 1935 saw the proclamation of the Nuremberg Laws and the abolition of all citizenship rights for Jews. Three years later, at 1.20 a.m. on 10 November 1938, came the infamous 'Kristallnacht' ('Night of Broken Glass'), when Jewish premises were broken into, synagogues burnt down, and heads of families taken away, never to return.

President Roosevelt, foreseeing the possibility of Jews fleeing this persecution, convened an international conference at Evian near the shores of Lake Geneva to discuss the rescue of Jewish refugees from Nazi Germany. Its outcome reveals the selfish caution of most of the countries present (including Ireland): 'Only the Dutch, the Danes and the Dominican Republic agreed to let in Jewish refugees without

8   Ibid., p. 117.

restrictions.'[9] The following year, another tragic incident highlights this same attitude:

> On 13 May 1939, the German transatlantic liner, *St Louis*, sailed from Hamburg for Havana, Cuba. Most of the 937 passengers were Jews fleeing the Nazis. They planned to remain in Cuba until the US visas they had applied for were issued. The Jews held landing certificates issued by the Cuban Director-General of Immigration, but even before the *St Louis* arrived in Cuba, President Federigo Laredo Bru had revoked all landing documents. When the *St Louis* docked in Havana Harbour on 27 May 1939, the only passengers allowed to go ashore were six non-Jews and twenty-two Jews with valid entry documents. Five days later they were ordered out of Cuban waters and sailed to Florida. Roosevelt ignored the pleas of the passengers and the State Department refused to allow them to land. The ship had to return to Germany where, with the exception of a few escapees, they were eventually rounded up and sent to the death camps.[10]

Then, on 1 September 1939, the German army invaded Poland. Britain, as one of the guarantors of Poland's borders, declared war on Germany. World War II had begun. The Nazis then advanced into Scandinavia, the Netherlands and France, reaching Paris on 16 June 1940. All occupied countries were ordered to initiate Hitler's programme for exterminating the Jews. There was resistance from the northernmost countries such as Finland, Sweden, Denmark

9 Gilbert, *Israel: A History*, p. 95.
10 Taken from Holocaust Memorial Day programme (Dublin), 2007.

and Holland. The Finns successfully refused to implement these orders. The Swedes maintained neutrality by bargaining with their iron ore. King Christian of Denmark rode into Copenhagen wearing the 'yellow star' in protest and the Danes, taking the lead from their sovereign, rounded up their Jews and herded them all to safety in Sweden. The Dutch protested loudly against Hitler's policy, but they proved unable to save their Jewish population in the end. In France, on the other hand, the (autonomous) Vichy government, permitted to operate in the south after the fall of Paris, cooperated with Hitler, set up its own concentration camps and facilitated the transportation of Jews to Auschwitz. (There was a popular resistance movement in France too, however, and many French people hid their Jews.) The governments of Austria and Czechoslovakia (occupied before 1939) cooperated willingly with Hitler's 'Final Solution'.

Jews trying to escape saw Palestine as their only hope, but shortly before the war the British government issued a White Paper limiting the numbers of Jewish refugees permitted to enter Palestine. Throughout the war, British officials turned ships carrying would-be Jewish immigrants away from the port of Haifa. The 'Struma', with 769 Jewish refugees on board, was refused entry into Turkey in 1941 and, in spite of the fact that the authorities were warned that the ship was in a dangerous condition (with engine problems, overcrowding and a lack of adequate sanitary facilities) was sent out into the Black Sea, where a mysterious explosion killed all but one on board.

The Polish government went into exile in London but continued to receive information from the homeland. They published a report on the fate of Polish Jews, gleaned from information received from their own couriers working on the ground back home. It was not acted upon. In 1942 the governments of Britain and the US received definitive confirmation of the mass extermination of Jews, but repeated requests (by Jewish groups) that the railway tracks leading to the concentration camps be bombed were refused. Davies tells us that: 'Airforce officers insisted on the priority of their military and industrial targets. ... One official of the British Foreign Office minuted: "a disproportionate amount of time ... is wasted ... on these wailing Jews."'[11]

The silence of the Christian churches has raised many questions and has been discussed elsewhere by many students of the period, but it is worth mentioning here that much of the criticism directed against Pope Pius XII has been refuted by Rabbi David Dalin in *The Myth of Hitler's Pope*. He counters the accusation of the Pope's silence by reminding us that Pius' first encyclical (*Summi Pontificatus*) evoked this response in the front page of the *New York Times*: 'POPE CONDEMNS DICTATORS, TREATY VIOLATORS, RACISM', and he quotes Heinrich Mueller's statement: '[T]his encyclical is directed exclusively against Germany ...' The fact that the Allies chose to drop 88,000 copies of the encyclical on Germany is another indication of how well the Pope's message was understood. His Christmas message of 1941, which has been criticised as 'not forceful enough', received this analysis in the German foreign office:

> ... his speech is one long attack on everything we
> stand for ... He is clearly speaking on behalf of the
> Jews ... he is virtually accusing the German people
> of injustice towards the Jews and makes himself
> the mouthpiece of the Jewish war criminals.[12]

Leading Catholic churchmen like Cardinal Roncalli (later John XXIII) and Cardinal Palazzini (honored in Yad Vashem) responded in much the same words as those of Cardinal Montini (later Paul VI) when offered an award for what he

11 Davies, p. 1026.
12 Dalin, p. 73.

had done to save Jews: 'All I did was my duty. And besides I only acted upon orders from the Holy Father. Nobody deserves a medal for that.'[13]

Whether a great public outcry would have helped or not, we do not know, but one has to admit that it is not clear that there was any will for such an outcry within Germany. Some people feared that as Hitler became more confident and more aggressive, any condemnation might bring worse consequences for all concerned. While acknowledging the heroism of those individuals who stood out from the crowd, one would have to recognise, in hindsight, that the difficulties and responsibility of making decisions in such extreme circumstances were enormous. Perhaps it is more constructive for us now to focus on the fact that Catholic Christian Europe did not only remain silent, but actually participated in the effort to annihilate the Jewish race. Apart from the fact that there were Catholics in the Nazi Party and the SS (Hitler himself was originally a Catholic, though his Nazi doctrine contained nothing to associate it with that faith), many of the ingredients of the Nazi persecution of the Jews were there already in the Christian past.

The badge, the ghetto and the condemnation of Jewish blood were all part of that shameful history, and, as we have seen, most of the other so-called Christian countries of Europe pursued, at best, ambivalent policies towards the death camps during the war.

After the War

What is even harder to understand or excuse is that, unbelievable though it may seem, anti-Semitism did not end with the war. Chaim Herzog, an intelligence officer in the British army during the war (he had joined along with thirty thousand other Jews), was present at the post-war conference in Bergen Belsen (1945). He comments:

13 Ibid., p. 84.

> There was remarkably little compassion for the
> Jewish survivors. It was as if the authorities were
> saying, 'The war is over and there were some bad
> times, but now let's pretend that none of it ever
> happened, so we can all go back to normal life.' ...
> The problem for the Jews was that there was no
> normal life to go back to.[14]

Herzog decided to join the struggle to set up a Jewish
homeland. He found himself suddenly isolated. He says: 'I
had a tremendous internal conflict. Being a member of the
British army was a big part of my identity. One day I find
myself sitting in an officer's mess in British Army
Headquarters as a major, a big chief. The next day I was
suspect by every British soldier I passed, simply because I was
a Jew.'[15] This former British officer describes the policy of the
British Mandate as 'ordered repression' and goes on to say
that the British sided with the Arabs. In his opinion they were
influenced by romantic ideas of the Arabs stemming from the
story of Lawrence of Arabia, but also by considerations of oil.
The British historian Martin Gilbert tells of another factor:
'One of the reiterated questions repeatedly asked behind the
scenes in British official discussions in London was whether
the Jewish needs in Palestine could really be allowed to
endanger the wider British need for the support of the
Muslim world.'[16] The future of the Empire, particularly in
India, was occupying the minds of many British politicians
but in the meantime:

14 *Living History*, Blaine, WA: Phoenix, 1996, p. 67.
15 Ibid., p. 75.
16 Gilbert, p. 67.

European Jews were constantly trying to smuggle themselves into Palestine illegally. Boats carrying 'illegal' Jews 'home' would try to land. British naval vessels would lie in wait for them to get close to shore and then ram the boats. Many people drowned and many lives were lost. The survivors, who had escaped from the horrors of the German concentration camps, were now placed in concentration camps built by the British in Cyprus ... But even this human tragedy was less important to the British than their damned quotas.[17]

Leon Uris in his novel *Exodus* immortalised the story of the four thousand European Jews whose ship was refused entry into Palestine and eventually returned to its port of embarkation in Hamburg (destined for *refugee* camps in Germany!) until the US President Truman intervened. Two years after the war, on 29 November 1947, the General Assembly of the UN voted for the establishment of two states in Palestine, one Jewish and one Arab. When the vote was taken, Britain was one of the ten countries to abstain, in spite of her previous commitment to the Balfour Agreement.

Post-War Anti-Semitism

Poland
Pogroms continued in Poland, the most well known being those in Kielce and Cracow. In a book called *Neighbors*, the Polish-born professor Jan T. Gross tells of how Jewish survivors 'returned to their homeland to be vilified, terrorised and in some 1,500 instances, murdered'. His book includes

17 Herzog, *Living History*, p. 77.

this quote from the Polish-Jewish journalist Saul Shneiderman (written the day after the massacre in Kielce): 'The immense courtyard was still littered with blood-stained iron pipes, stones and clubs, which had been used to crush the skulls of Jewish men and women.' He also makes the following observations: Kielce was 'nothing special ... during this era it could have taken place anywhere in Poland'; 'Polish intellectuals were mortified by what was happening in their country.' Gross also informs us that, only days before the pogrom, Cardinal August Hlond had spurned Jewish entreaties to condemn Roman Catholic anti-Semitism and that afterwards he charged that, by leading the effort to impose Communism on Poland, the Jews had only themselves to blame.[18] Two additional waves of anti-Semitism in Poland (1956–57 and 1968–69) were inspired by the Soviet government, and these drove most of the remaining Polish Jews out of the country.

Russia
The Russian government supported the state of Israel at first, but during the Cold War changed its policy in order to gain the support of Arab and African countries. As the Soviet economy declined persecution of Jews intensified.

France
Raissa Maritain, herself born a Jew, complained about the fact that in her day men were persecuted as Jews, 'whose blood through two world wars was counted as French'. Nevertheless, the government did restrain anti-Semitism up until the Six Day War (1967). A remark by Charles de Gaulle on that occasion (which referred to the Jews as 'a domineering people sure of itself') is said to have sparked the rash of desecration of Jewish cemeteries that followed. Bombings aimed at Jews

18 *Neighbors*, Princeton University Press, 2001.

were carried out in 1975 and 1980 until finally, when a bomb thrown at the Simchat Torah synagogue killed four Jews and injured twenty others, there was public outrage and protestors took to the streets demanding that the government take action.[19]

Egypt

Egypt became a refuge for Nazi war criminals who were welcomed there. One of these was a man named Haj Amin al-Husseini. He had been appointed Grand Mufti of Jerusalem by the British in 1922 but organised a rebellion against the British Mandate in 1936. A strong supporter of the Nazi cause, he received an invitation to Berlin from Hitler himself at the beginning of the war, and not only did he meet Hitler personally on that occasion, but he spent the duration of the war in Berlin working with Eichmann and Himmler, becoming a personal friend of the latter. When he landed in Egypt in 1945 he met up with a young relative, Yasser Arafat, and became his teacher and mentor. Arafat succeeded him as leader of the Palestinian Liberation Organisation in 1965.

USA

As already mentioned, Russia looked to the Arab countries for support during the Cold War, and the US supported Israel – in turn benefiting from their ally in the Middle East. Nevertheless there was anti-Semitism there too. In the 1960s, six hundred synagogues were desecrated and discrimination in housing and schooling was reintroduced. The Black Caucus consistently supported Israel and the Civil Rights Movement was strongly supported by Jewish leadership, but there was a rise in black anti-Semitism between the years 1964 and 1981. The Six Day War of 1967 was first hailed as the ingenious victory of a small nation over massive Arab forces, but a

19 Flannery, p. 280.

different mood emerged soon after. Writing in 1980, Flannery, an American, said of this time: '... a number of socialist and radical groups have mounted an almost frenzied attack on Israel and Zionism ...'[20] He continues: 'The tendency to support the Arab position and treat Israel severely has been detected also in liberal circles, religious as well as secular. Anti-Semitism's turn to the Left has been a wide one.'[21] He explains how many see Israel as 'the out-post of American capitalism and imperialism ... which stands in the way not only of the Palestinian people, but of development and liberation in the Third World' whereas the truth is that 'Israel, sole democracy in the Middle East, is an independent, egalitarian, and moderately socialist state that has offered and provided technological and agricultural aid to the Third World countries whenever asked to do so, and that seeks a lasting peace and co-operation with its Arab neighbours'.[22]

South America
Nazi criminals were welcomed by the government of Argentina, and Jewish communities in Brazil, Chile and Uruguay suffered attacks on their synagogues and other anti-Semitic incidents in the 1960s and 1970s.

Despite this bleak record there was, and there is, a more hopeful side to this story. As more and more information emerged about the deliberate, cold-blooded plan to extinguish the entire Jewish population of Europe, and the near success of that plan (approximately six million people were killed out of a total of nine and a half million), many individuals and churches began a process of soul searching. How could such an evil plan have been conceived and carried out within the borders of 'Christian' Europe? The results of

20 Ibid., p. 274.
21 Ibid., p. 275.
22 Ibid., p. 276.

the soul-searching, which took place in the Catholic Church, and the hope that the subsequent changes in her teaching afford, will be recounted in the final chapter of this book. But first we need to look at our own country and its record in this dreadful saga.

CHAPTER SIX

Ireland and the Jews

> This country has long been honourably
> distinguished by its tolerance towards the Jews ...
> not ignorant of persecution and its evils, our own
> race ought to be especially careful to avoid its
> infliction.[1]

The Jewish Museum in Dublin displays a short extract from
the Annals of Innisfallen. This extract tells of five or six Jews
who came to Ireland to visit King Tordelbach in 1062. They
were sent away, but since the next entry records the chieftain's
visit to Jerusalem the following year, the writer suggests that
'perhaps they only came to promote tourism'!

Jews, however, were officially welcomed to England by
William the Conqueror about 1066, and in the opinion of
Chaim Herzog (who lived in Dublin from 1918 to 1934), there
was probably a small Jewish community in Dublin during the
Middle Ages. It is certain that some of the Jews exiled from
Spain and Portugal at the end of the fifteenth century
eventually landed in Ireland and that the first synagogue in
Dublin was built by Portuguese Jews in 1660. From that time
on, a small Jewish community lived in Dublin (around Mary's
Abbey, north of the Liffey) up until the nineteenth century.
There is no record of animosity or of any incidents against

---

1   From the *Cork Examiner*, quoted in *Jewish Chronicle*, 25 April 1884.

them. In fact Ireland acquired a reputation for tolerance in relation to the Jews.

In the year 1747 or thereabouts, the Irish House of Commons, rebuking an anti-Jewish outbreak in England, openly condemned such unchristian violence and extended a welcome to the oppressed Jews to the shelter of the land of Ireland.[2] In 1787 the Irish House of Commons passed a resolution for the naturalisation of all Jews who wished to become Irish citizens. When the parliament was dissolved and Irish members were obliged to attend Westminster, Daniel O'Connell pioneered a campaign for Catholic Emancipation and was elected MP for Clare in 1828. At that time Rabbi Isaac Goldsmid sent to Ireland to secure O'Connell's support for the introduction of a Bill to remove Jewish civil disabilities. O'Connell responded with these words: 'Ireland has claims on your ancient race, and it is the only Christian country that I know of unsullied by any acts of persecution against the Jews.' Referring to the principle of the freedom of conscience, he continued: '… and no man can admit the sacred principle without extending it to the Jew as to the Christian.'[3]

In 1892, when Rabbi Adler, Chief Rabbi of the British Empire, presided at the consecration of the new synagogue at Adelaide Road, he addressed his people with these words: 'Brethren, you have come from a country like unto Egypt of old, to a land which offers you hospitality and shelter. It is said that Ireland is the only country in the world which cannot be charged with persecuting the Jews.'[4]

2 Michael Davitt's letter to the *Freeman's Journal* in *Limerick Boycott 1904*, by Dermot Keogh and Andrew McCarthy, Cork: Mercier Press, 2005, p. 43.

3 Dermot Keogh, *Jews in Twentieth Century Ireland*, Cork University Press, 1998, p. 7.

4 Ibid., p. 19.

The Limerick 'Boycott' (1904)

The pogroms following the assassination of the Czar of Russia (1881) saw two million Jews flee that country. A large number of these refugees arrived in Britain, and from there some came to Ireland. Most of these settled in Dublin near the South Circular Road, in an area later known as 'Little Jerusalem'. A few hundred arrived in Cobh and from there some moved on to Cork and Limerick. There were 130 Jews living in Limerick by 1896.[5] Louis Goldberg was one of those who escaped the pogroms in Lithuania in 1882. He was about thirteen years old when he arrived in Cobh, where he was befriended by a fellow Jew who provided him with accommodation for a few nights. From there he walked to Dublin, where he borrowed ten shillings from another friendly Jew. He bought some small articles with the money, which he peddled on his return journey. He then made his way to Limerick, where some other Jews put him up until such time as he earned enough money to rent a room for himself. This story is typical of many of the new immigrants. Penniless but prepared to work hard in all weathers, they soon became independent. Sometimes the newcomers had to endure name-calling from children, but some of them testified to the kindness of local individuals.[6]

Rabbi Elias Levin, speaking in 1904, said of the previous quarter of a century that Jewish families in the city of Limerick had lived 'in perfect peace and harmony with their Christian neighbours of all classes'.[7] Imagine their surprise then when, out of the blue, one evening in January of that year a mob converged outside their homes and businesses ready to attack. This angry crowd had come straight from a sermon on the occasion of a meeting of the Archconfraternity

5   Ibid., xi.
6   Ibid.
7   Keogh and McCarthy, *Limerick Boycott 1904*.

of the Holy Family. The preacher was the new director, a young Redemptorist priest named Fr Creagh, a native of Limerick who had returned only shortly before. It appears that after his arrival he was approached by some local traders, who said they were concerned about the competition they were facing from Jewish pedlars. The priest took the opportunity of his first meeting with the men's sodality to address the subject. It was said of him at the time that he was a 'charismatic' speaker and that 'his preaching was irresistible ... he spared no one and the people just loved it, regularly overflowing the church into the street'.[8] He began by telling the people that the Jews were responsible for enslaving them to usury. Pointing to a newspaper account of a recent Jewish wedding, he asked how the Jews could afford such a celebration. Noting the clothing of those in attendance and comparing the apparent prosperity of those who wore them with the poverty of the native Irish, he went on to say that 'they killed Christ', even adding the old libels of ritual murder and naming a number of so-called 'martyr victims'. In conclusion he advised those present to avoid doing business with the Jews and to stop now if they had already started to do so. This advice was repeated the following week in yet another sermon that, though denouncing violence, still continued the verbal attack on the Jews.[9]

Mr. J. Blond, a merchant, forced by the campaign that followed to sell out his trading stock, wrote to *The Times* on 10 April 1904 saying:

> It took me all these years, with the greatest pain and trouble and working unceasingly until I had established myself comfortably and enjoyed a nice trade, until, all of a sudden, like a thunderstorm,

8   Ibid., p. 27.
9   Keogh, *Jews in Twentieth Century Ireland*, pp. 35 and 36.

spoke hatred and animosity against the Jews, how
they crucified Lord Jesus, how they martyred St
Simon, and gradually in one month's time, I have
none of my previous customers coming into my
shop. In fact, my business is nil at present. Would
you call my trade a national evil? I defy anyone in
this city to say whom I have wronged, what did I
overcharge ... since the beginning of the crusade
of Fr Creagh against the Jews we never got a fair
chance to defend ourselves or to put our case
rightly before the Public.[10]

The official report for Dublin Castle of the effect of the
'boycott' on the Jews of Limerick was filed by District
Inspector O'Hara on 12 March 1904: 'The police now report
that within the past year, eight Jewish families (forty-nine
persons) have left Limerick. Of these, five families left because
of the "agitation" ... They ... number thirty-two persons.
Twenty-six families remain, of whom eight only are in good
circumstances.'[11]

There were violent incidents associated with these events
too, but thankfully no fatalities. The fear engendered in the
Jewish community, however, was very real. These eastern
European Jews had plenty of experience of this kind of
hostility in the past, as well as vivid recollections suggesting
how it might develop. A special correspondent for the *Jewish
Chronicle*, reporting from the city on 18 January 1905, gives
us an inkling of how they must have felt:

The miserable cry: 'Down with the Jews', 'Death
to the Jews', 'We hunt them out' is still ringing in
my ears, and sends a cold shiver through my body.
Today, Monday, the chief business of the day, Jews

10 Ibid., p. 49.
11 Ibid., p. 51.

were attacked right and left. I myself witnessed one scene where a Jew was actually running for his life, and as he passed through one crowd he was actually hemmed in by another, till the police came on the scene. But that is only one case out of many! And this in a land of freedom, this in the twentieth century, this only two weeks after Christmas, when peace and goodwill to all mankind was preached throughout the land! ... When I witnessed the organised attacks today and heard the mob yell 'Down with the Jews! They kill innocent children', all the horrors of Kishineff [referring to the 1903 pogrom in Kishinev Beeserabia, Russia] came back to me, and then, and only then, was I able to realise what Kishineff meant.[12]

Michael Davitt, founder of the Land League, wrote angrily to the editor of the *Freeman's Journal* about the whole incident: 'Irish Catholics have suffered every form of religious oppression known to the perverted ingenuity of the authors of the penal code, but it is their proud boast that neither in Ireland nor in any land to which English rule has forced them to fly did they ever resort to a counter religious persecution.' Referring to the preacher's claim that 'nowadays they dare not kidnap and slay Christian children', he wrote:

Sir, it was atrocious language like this, which, in May last, was responsible for some of the most hideous crimes possible to perverted humanity, in a Russian city [referring to Kishinev]. There is not an atom of truth in the horrible allegations of

12 Keogh and McCarthy, p. 35.

ritual murder here insinuated against this persecuted race.

He reminded his readers that the popes of the Middle Ages condemned this libel and further added:

> I protest, as a Christian and as a Catholic, against the spirit of barbarous malignity being introduced into Ireland, under the pretended form of a material regard for the welfare of our workers.[13]

John Redmond, leader of the Irish Parliamentary Party, wrote to the local rabbi Levin: 'I have no sympathy whatever with the attacks on the Hebrew community in Limerick or elsewhere. I feel sure that the good sense and toleration of the Irish people will be sufficient to protect them from any wrong.'[14] But unfortunately this was not the only view on the political spectrum. Arthur Griffith, whose paper *The United Irishman* expressed anti-Semitic views during the Dreyfus Affair, wrote himself in 1899: 'I have in former years often declared that the Three Evil Influences of the century were the Pirate, the Freemason and the Jew.' The paper declared that its sympathy went out to:

> ... our countrymen, the artisans whom the Jew deprives of the means of livelihood ... In short, our sympathy is so much drained by that dreary weekly procession of our own flesh and blood out of Ireland that we have none left to bestow on the weekly procession of aliens coming in.[15]

13 Ibid., p. 43.
14 Ibid., p. 44.
15 Ibid., p. 65.

The Catholic press (influenced, no doubt, by events in France) expressed the same kind of views in the course of the controversy. Fr Finlay SJ, managing editor of the university magazine *Lyceum*, for example, wrote an article full of innuendo and insinuations about the Jews and their trading, but when an investigation into his accusations were carried out on orders coming from the Castle they were found to be completely false.

Michael Davitt recommended to Rabbi Levin that he seek a meeting with the Catholic bishop Dr Thomas O'Dwyer. The bishop declined to meet him but communicated with him through his secretary, requesting that the Rabbi not speak to the press. Fr Mathias Raus, Superior General of the Redemptorists (the Congregation to which Fr Creagh belonged) visited Limerick later that year. The Rabbi sought a meeting with him also, but was again denied.

The Provincial journal of the Redemptorists had this to say: 'a former consultor general, Fr Magnier, and the provincial, Fr Boylan ... were with Fr Creagh on his attack on the Jews and consequently Fr Creagh continued his campaign against the Jews.' The same source added that: 'Bishop O'Dwyer was certainly not defending the Jews, but he was offended because he was not asked beforehand about the sermons attacking the Jews.'[16]

The local people in Limerick at this time were extremely poor. What little industry there had been in the town was almost all gone. Alcohol abuse was an issue (another topic of concern to the Confraternity at the time), and was, of course, a drain on whatever money there was about. People had little hope of bettering themselves. Fr Creagh, with all the authority his priestly position commanded in the Ireland of the day, set a flame to the embers of unrest and discontent.

16 Ibid., p. 60.

Ostensibly, one could say that the relative prosperity of the Jews raised questions. They had come to the country only a short time previously and were already better clothed than many of the local Irish. These Jews, however, had centuries of experience of having to find new ways of making a living. They were therefore both inventive and enterprising. Moreover, throughout the years of persecution Jewish communities, as a whole, maintained high standards of discipline, centred on the study of Torah. This was especially true in eastern Europe where these Jews came from. They were thrifty and hard-working and there is no evidence of any other reason for their relative success.

It must be noted, however, that not all the Jews left Limerick after 1904 and that the Jewish community actually continued to grow up until the late 1920s. The decline set in after, so that by the early 1940s only two Jewish families (Fine and Clein) remained. We shall see that towards the end of the century an effort was made by the local community to make a gesture of friendship to the Irish Jews, an offer graciously accepted by them.

Fr Creagh was never publicly condemned in Ireland, a fact commented on in the English press. The whole sorry incident is reminiscent of the Middle Ages, and the unwillingness of Church authorities to openly condemn the victimisation of the Jews on this occasion, for whatever reason, can only be deemed reprehensible.

Some writers have been at pains to point out that the opposition to the Jews in Limerick at this time had nothing to do with their religious beliefs but only with their practice of money-lending. It is true that Fr Creagh did focus on the issue of usury, but he failed to observe that there were Christian usurers operating there also at this time.

From the perspective of this study, the significance of the whole event is the ease with which the feelings of the people were roused and Ireland's reputation for good relations with

Jews suddenly ceased to exist. The Jewish people were at risk in Ireland after only one inflammatory sermon, just as had been the case in numerous other European countries so often before.

Attitudes in Ireland between the Two Wars

The climate in the 1920s (as experienced by the Jews) can be gleaned from the writing of Chaim Herzog, as he describes his early years in Dublin:

> On many occasions stones were thrown at us by young urchins who believed that this was the best way to settle the account with the Jewish people for allegedly crucifying Christ. Ireland had no history of anti-Semitism and while I did not feel outcast, I did feel different. I was always aware that somewhere in the background I was being judged by different standards. When a Jew was arrested for a crime, the entire Jewish community shuddered, because it was expected that all Jews would be thought guilty of that crime.[17]

But by now anti-Semitism was growing in the country, and as on the continent this brand of anti-Semitism was more connected with nationalism than with either religion or economics.

Eoin O'Duffy embarrassed his own party of Fine Gael by organising the 'Blue Shirts' and holding anti-Semitic rallies around the country. Charles Bewley, another anti-Semite, was appointed Ireland's envoy to Germany in 1933. (Reports full of praise for Nazi Germany were sent back to Ireland, but the authorities gradually became dissatisfied with his work and he was removed from office in 1939.)

17 Herzog, p. 9.

Another feature of this time was the presence in the country of Nazi personnel. Dr Adolf Mahr, keeper of the Irish Antiquities division of the National Museum from September 1927, was appointed director of the museum in 1934. (Frederick Boland, assistant secretary of the Department of External Affairs, described him as 'the most active and fanatical National Socialist in the German colony here'.) The manager of the Turf Board, Heinz Mecking, was a Nazi, as was Colonel Wilhelm Fritz Brase, director of the Army School of Music. Then there were the religious fanatics, such as Fathers Denis Fahey and Edward Cahill SJ, both professors of theology, and prolific writers who:

> ... both depicted the Jew as being responsible for the moral corruption of western society and for the fomenting of world revolution. Fahey was also ever mindful of the alleged hidden hand of Jews in the economic, political, and moral subversion of Irish society.[18]

These were worrying trends, but it would seem nevertheless that they did not pervade the entire society. There were some enlightened voices. The historian Dr T.W. Moody, for example, took exception to the views of the Catholic press and wrote a pamphlet for the Catholic Truth Society entitled 'Why are the Jews persecuted?' (1938). This quote from the pamphlet highlights the kind of criticism that was being applied to Jews at the time:

> To deny the actuality of the forces which determined the formation of the Jewish soul is to deny the obvious testimony of history. To pass

18 Keogh, p. 92.

strict moral judgement upon a people who have been bred in the bitter cauldron of hate and oppression is to neglect the basic laws of justice and charity. It is far more reasonable to try to understand the modern Jew in the light of the conditions which have shaped him. Nor is it beside the point to insist that not only is this the rational view, but it is the only one consistent with the high principles of our Christian faith.[19]

Two other enlightened men who were concerned about the ignorant and potentially dangerous attitudes abroad were Frank Duff, founder of the Legion of Mary, and his friend Leoin O'Broin. Keogh says that they were '... very sensitive to the ignorance, the ambivalence, and the prejudice towards the Jews to be found in much Irish popular Catholic literature'.[20] Duff and O'Broin set up an organisation, the object of which was to facilitate dialogue with Jews, calling it 'The Pillar of Fire'. But when the Archbishop of Dublin John Charles McQuaid intervened to make the stipulation that Catholics only (and preferably clerics) be allowed to present talks at their meetings, the two organisers decided to disband rather than subject their Jewish friends to this insult.

The War Years

Nevertheless, despite this degree of anti-Semitism, it must have seemed to many Jews before the war that Ireland would be a good place to seek refuge. Isaac Herzog was Chief Rabbi of Dublin from 1918 to 1937. He had been an open supporter of the Irish cause during the War of Independence and had become a personal friend of Éamon de Valera, even giving him the security of a safe house on one occasion. Robert

19 Ibid., p. 97.
20 Ibid., p. 96.

Briscoe was a popular and active member of the Dáil and also a personal friend of de Valera, having taken his side during the Civil War. Dr Isaac Herzog was appointed Chief Rabbi of Palestine in 1937 and in this capacity wrote on numerous occasions to de Valera (now the Taoiseach) requesting help for Jews in danger of the death camps. The answer came repeatedly that de Valera would do all he could 'as leader of a neutral country'.

It is not clear how many Jews were actually afforded asylum in Ireland but it is acknowledged that they were very few. Gerald Goldberg tells of an episode in Cork during 1939 in which he was involved. It concerned a German Jew who jumped ship at Cobh, and was given permission by a friendly customs official to come ashore. The man's family had been forced to split up because of Nazi persecution and he was in danger of being arrested if deported. All efforts to get asylum status for him failed, including a direct appeal to de Valera. The unfortunate man was deported back to Germany and spent the rest of the war in a concentration camp.[21]

Another refusal is recorded in a copy of a letter carrying a Rathmines address, which was sent to the authorities in Dublin on 14 February 1938. In it the writer requests permission to bring his twenty-three-year-old niece from Poland to Ireland. (Her mother was a widow and the writer himself undertakes to provide for the girl and, in particular, not to send her to work, given the unemployment problem.) The reply is as follows:

> I am directed by the Minister for Justice to state that he regrets that he does not see his way to grant permission to you to bring your niece ... a Polish national, to this country for the purpose of permanent residence.

21 Taken from Holocaust Memorial Day programme (Dublin), 2006.

The young woman in question was murdered, along with the rest of her family, in the Holocaust.[22]

News of the death camps in Germany was confirmed and relayed to the British government in 1942 and that information was passed to the Irish government in March of that year. Two TDs, Paddy Belton and Oliver J. Flanagan, had already been on record in the 1930s making anti-Semitic statements in the Dáil, but as late as 1943, after news of the death camps had already reached this country, Dáil records show the following statement by Oliver Flanagan as he addressed the Taoiseach:

> There is one thing that Germany did, and that was to rout the Jews out of their country. Until we rout the Jews out of this country, it does not matter a hair's breadth what orders you make. Where the bees are there is honey, and where the Jews are there is money.[23]

However, it was not the TDs but the Civil Service who were to the forefront in opposing asylum to the Jews. Keogh tells us: 'The Department of Justice's interpretation of policy remained consistent throughout the war; the admission of Jews was to be generally discouraged ...'[24] As more papers are released on the basis of the State's Secret Act, this conclusion has been strongly confirmed.

As late as 1953, eight years after the war, Robert Briscoe TD was still experiencing great difficulty as he tried to find a home for ten Jewish families in Ireland. The response of the Department of Justice was as follows:

22 Ibid.
23 Dáil Eireann, Proceedings, 1943. (Flanagan later apologised for these remarks.)
24 Keogh, p. 161.

> [I]n the administration of the alien laws it has
> always been recognised in the Department of
> Justice, Industry and Commerce and External
> Affairs, that the question of the admission of
> aliens of Jewish blood presents a special problem
> and the alien laws have been administered less
> liberally in their case.[25]

Even the intervention of de Valera and his government gained only the acceptance of five of the ten families. The statement from the Department of Justice, Industry and Commerce is all the more shameful when we remember that only a short time before, in the late 1930s and when Irish interests dictated it, Jewish businessmen were being encouraged to come to Ireland to set up factories. (Seán Lemass himself spearheaded a delegation to Europe to investigate such possibilities and as a result three factories were set up in the west of the country by Jewish businessmen, providing employment to locals for years.)

Dr Keogh's conclusion that de Valera sincerely wished to help the Jews and tried all the diplomatic channels open to him may well be correct, but neither de Valera nor anyone else took any bold or courageous initiatives, as was done in some other countries, to come to the rescue of the Jews. (For example, and as already noted, Sweden was also a neutral country, but still took all the refugees rescued by the Danes.) On the contrary, it would seem that an inordinate amount of time was spent on consultation and correspondence in a moment of dire need, and that neither Church nor State took any strong action.

It could be argued that the administrative system, the model of which this country chose to inherit from the British,

25 Ibid., p. 222.

accorded too much power to the civil service. (Secretaries of departments in Ireland remained in office at that time, regardless of the departure of ministers, a practice that had been discontinued in Britain.) But no matter what excuse we offer, as a country so recently freed from oppression itself we must surely agree that it is to our shame that we could dally around while those on whom 'Ireland has claims' (Daniel O'Connell) were annihilated in their millions.

As the century progressed consciences began to stir in some places at least. In the early 1970s, the county manager in Limerick, Richard Haslam, discovered that the Jewish cemetery had been neglected and began the process which resulted in its restoration and maintenance. The completion of this work was marked by an ecumenical service celebrated in 1990, attended by the Chief Rabbi and both the Catholic and Church of Ireland bishops. This small act, it was said, meant much to members of the Jewish community. The Chief Rabbi, referring to the ceremony itself as well as to the history of the Jews in Limerick, made the following statement: 'This is a significant but sad occasion, for while we recall a period of bitterness and suffering endured by Jewish inhabitants of the city a few generations ago, we gather today in a wonderful spirit of fraternity, harmony and peace.'[26]

But as yet Ireland had not faced up to its failure to help the Jews during the war and it was not until 1995, on the occasion of the first Holocaust Memorial in Ireland, that the then Taoiseach, John Bruton, acknowledged with regret that Ireland had not lived up to its reputation of tolerance towards the Jews in their hour of greatest need. On the occasion of the first Holocaust Memorial Day (2003) the then Minister for Justice, Michael McDowell, again acknowledged the failure of this state and of the Irish people to honour our own constitution and the rights it guarantees to the Jewish community:

26 Keogh, p. 53.

> (a) By tolerating social discrimination; (b) by failing to heed the message of the persecuted, or ... offer refuge to those who sought it; and (c) by failing to confront those who openly or covertly offered justification for the prejudice and race hatred which led to the Shoah.[27]

Since then, the Irish government has set up a national charity known as the Holocaust Educational Trust with Ruairi Quinn TD as its chairperson. The government has begun to take steps to repair our deplorable record. The Church, at the highest level (as we shall see in the next chapter) has not been inactive either, but there is little evidence of this on the ground as yet.

27 Holocaust Memorial Day 2003. For Jewish people, the term 'Shoah' (disaster) is preferable to 'Holocaust' since the latter is a religious term.

CHAPTER SEVEN

Repentance, Redemption, Hope

The most unnoticed of all miracles is the miracle of repentance ... It is not the same thing as rebirth; it is transformation, creation ... In the dimension of time there is no going back ... [but]... the power of repentance causes time to be created backward and allows recreation of the past to take place ... Through the forgiving hand of God, harm and blemish which we have committed against the world and against ourselves will be extinguished, transformed into salvation. God brings about this creation for the sake of humanity when a human being repents for the sake of God.[1]

The person who knows how to acknowledge the truth of guilt, and asks Christ for forgiveness enhances his own human dignity and manifests spiritual greatness.[2]

That a plan such as the 'Final Solution' could have been devised within the borders of a continent that boasted a long

1   Rabbi Abraham Heschel, 'The Meaning of Repentance', *Moral Grandeur and Spiritual Audacity: Essays of Rabbi Abraham Heschel*, Susannah Heschel (ed.), New York: Farrar, 1996, p. 69.
2   Pope John Paul II, Homily, Phoenix Park, 1979.

tradition of Christianity clearly demonstrated that something was gravely wrong. Thinking Christians could not avoid the issue. How could so many people who called themselves Christians have collaborated with the Nazi regime, ignored the atrocities committed, and treated the situation as if it were no concern of theirs?

Jules Isaac, a Jewish historian, author of the book *Jesus et Israel*, and survivor of Nazi oppression, set about looking for a way to promote respect for his people among Christians. While studying theology and engaging in biblical research, his friend Malcolm Hay, a Catholic and student of Hebrew and of Jewish culture, advised him to seek an audience with the Pope, John XXIII, to discuss his difficulties with Catholic teaching relating to Jews and Judaism.

Archbishop Angello Roncalli was elected Pope John XXIII in 1958. He had been the Vatican's apostolic delegate to Istanbul during World War II and had played a key role in helping Hungarian Jews to escape and also in getting papal help for the Jews of Transnistria – a Romanian-administered province made up of territories seized from the Soviet Union in 1941. In all of this he had worked closely with the Chief Rabbi of Palestine, Dr Isaac Herzog. The Rabbi later said of him: 'Cardinal Roncalli is a man who really loves the People of the Book, and through him thousands of Jews were rescued.'[3]

From the beginning of his pontificate, the reality of his love for 'the People of the Book' was borne out. One of his first actions was to remove offensive references to Jews from the solemn prayers of the Catholic Liturgy and from the prayer for the dedication of the world to the Sacred Heart. When receiving a delegation of Jewish leaders from America in 1960 (they came to thank him for his work in saving Turkish Jews during the Nazi persecution), Pope John (whose Christian name was Giuseppe) chose to greet them with the biblical

3   Dalin, p. 95.

words, 'I am Joseph your brother' (Genesis 45:3), a gesture greatly appreciated.

The Pope received Jules Isaac in private audience on 13 June 1960, and Isaac presented him with some of his writings, including a list of topics for clarification, or correction, by the teaching authority of the Church. He was the first to refer to the teaching of the Church regarding the Jews as 'the teaching of contempt' – a phrase later owned and used by Cardinal Johannes Willebrands.[4] Prior to this meeting, Pope John had already announced his intention of convening an ecumenical council. In preparation for that event he had appointed Cardinal Bea head of the Secretariat for Christian Unity and gave him the task of preparing a Declaration on the Jewish People to be submitted to the council. The Pope suggested that Isaac meet with Cardinal Bea. (It is significant that a Declaration on the Jewish People was part of the task of the Secretariat for Christian Unity. Pope John Paul II makes the same connection in 'Ecclesia in Europa', Rome, 2003, when he says: 'It is necessary to encourage dialogue with Judaism, knowing that it is fundamentally important for the self-knowledge of Christians and for the transcending of divisions between the churches and to work for a flowering of a new spring time in mutual relations.')

The plan for a Declaration on the Jewish People to be submitted to a General Council is without precedent in the two-thousand-year history of the Church and marks a distinct change in the Church's attitude to the Jewish people. Moreover, since the writings of the Fathers of the Church belong to that period of tension and struggle between the first Christians and the Jews and reflect their negative anti-Semitic views, this work would have to be accomplished without reference to them. These ancient works would have been the

4 'The Church facing Modern Anti-Semitism', lecture given by Johannes Cardinal Willebrands at Malcolm Hay Memorial, Aberdeen University, 17 October 1988.

natural reference point from which the Council fathers could begin. Now, however, they had to be ignored, a decision that underlines in bold print the sincerity and honesty with which the Catholic Church was embarking on its path of change and renewal. The commitment to such serious soul-searching is surely a manifestation of the presence of God's Spirit in and with the Church. The extraordinary fidelity with which the recommendations of the Council would be carried out subsequently by Pope Paul VI and more especially by Pope John Paul II adds even more strength to that hopeful impression.

It is worth noting that when Cardinal Bea's draft paper on the subject of the Jews was put on hold during the preparations for the Council (because of political issues in Arab-Israeli relations), the Pope intervened personally to have it put back on the agenda.

The Second Vatican Council

Vatican II formally opened on 11 October 1962. *Lumen gentium* (the Dogmatic Constitution on the Church) was one of the most important of all the documents that emerged from the Council. It includes the following statement:

> That people to whom the promises and covenants were made, and from which Christ was born according to the flesh (Rom 9:4-5), in view of the divine choice, are a people most dear because of the fathers, for the gifts of God are without repentance (Rom 2:28-29).[5]

This statement represents a return to the thinking of St Paul, and a clear move away from the accepted understanding

5   *Lumen gentium*, 16.

handed down in the Middle Ages i.e. 'the Jews bear responsibility for the death of Christ and must suffer forever on that account'. The acknowledgment that 'the gifts of God are without repentance' challenges the other notion of replacement theology taught by St Augustine and other Fathers of the Church.

In October 1965 the document *Nostra aetate* was passed by a large majority (though not without some strong opposition).[6] In its entirety the document deals with the Church and non-Christian religions. Of particular note here is the Council's proclamation concerning the Jews. Of them it states: that Christians and Jews are all alike children of Abraham; that we, Christians, received the revelation of the Old Testament through the Jews; and that we continue to be nourished from the good olive tree of Judaism (Romans XI).

The Council Fathers also highlighted the Jewishness of Jesus, Mary and the Apostles and declared unequivocally that the Jews, far from being 'accursed', are very dear to God. They pointed out that neither 'all Jews at the time of the passion nor Jews today' can be held responsible for the crimes committed during the suffering and death of Jesus but that, on the contrary, all of humanity carries responsibility in respect of Christ's Passion and Death. They encouraged dialogue between Catholics and Jews, another very important step. No longer are we told to fear 'Judaising', but rather we are encouraged to be enriched by the faith of our elder brethren.[7]

It is a sad reflection on the realities of our times, however, that the Council Fathers had to recall at this point too the

6 In this context, see extract from the obituary of Sr Rose Thering OP, published in *The Tablet*, Summer 2006, which is reproduced on p. 145.
7 *Nostra aetate*, 4.

dangers Jewish people may still face, even from those who consider themselves loyal members of the Church, and so they clearly state that: '... the Church deplores all hatred, persecution, displays of anti-Semitism leveled at any time and from any source at the Jews ...' They also remind us all that, on the contrary, Christians carry a serious responsibility to proclaim the Cross as the sign of God's universal love and source of all grace.

Years later Pope John Paul II would describe *Nostra aetate* as 'the decisive turning point in the relations between the Catholic Church and Judaism.' On the twentieth anniversary of this Declaration on the Jewish People, Rabbi Mardochei Waxman, in an address to a Jewish-Catholic assembly at the Vatican, stated:

> October 1965 was both a historic and a revolutionary date. It marked a turning away from eighteen centuries often characterised by misunderstanding and persecution, toward a dialogue in which we explored our common spiritual roots and confronted our disagreements frankly, but in a spirit of mutual understanding and respect.[8]

Back in 1965, however, the document was a disappointment to the Jewish people. They did not believe themselves that they bore any responsibility for the death of Jesus, but they had hoped that the Council would accept some Catholic responsibility for the sufferings inflicted on Jews throughout the ages and express some regret for it. Their reaction was understandable (it seems that Pope John was also disappointed), but in hindsight one can see that a step was

8   Michael Maher, 'Roman Catholics and Jews since the Holocaust', *Milltown Studies*, 53, 2004, p. 189.

taken which, given the history that went before it, was in the right direction.

Christians and Muslims in the Arab world were not enthusiastic either. They condemned the statement as representing a 'pro-Israeli' position. Some conservative Catholics passed anti-Semitic pamphlets into the Council voicing their objections. But the Council Fathers were firm in their stance and they had the goodwill of Jews with them. Soon after the conclusion of the Council, structures were set up, both in the Catholic and Jewish communities, to enable meetings to take place between members of both faiths. In 1970 a permanent International Liaison Committee between the Roman Catholic Church and the World Jewish community was created in Rome by Pope Paul VI. Issues of anti-Semitism were given first place on the agenda.

Paul VI also created the Commission for Religious Relations with the Jews. Dealing with anti-Semitism, which it repeatedly condemned, was part of the Commission's agenda, but it also had responsibility for what was an entirely new development in the history of both faiths. The Commission published 'Guidelines on Religious Relations with Jews' in which it acknowledged the validity of Jewish commitment to the Covenant between God and his People, affirmed the lasting value of the Hebrew Bible, and encouraged Catholics to appreciate the richness and vitality of the Jewish faith today. The guidelines marked a significant change in the Church's attitude to the Jews.

In 1978, John Paul II was elected Pope. The first ever Polish Pope, and one who had witnessed at first hand the evils of the Shoah (Holocaust), he was surely a highly significant choice from the point of view of the Jews, a point maybe not initially appreciated.

Prior to the war, Poland was the country with the highest density of European Jews, and as Davies says: 'No European country was more scarred by the Holocaust ... Jewry's thousand-year Polish abode came to an end.'[9] The new Pope's intimate knowledge of Jews and their suffering, especially during the Nazi period, strongly influenced his pontificate. Only a few months into that pontificate (March 1979), Pope John Paul met with Jewish representatives attending a meeting in Rome. He acknowledged at this audience the 'friendly response and good will, indeed the cordial initiative that the Church has found and continues to find among large sections of the Jewish community'. He also made a commitment to those present: 'I intend to foster spiritual dialogue and to do everything in my power for the peace of that land which is holy for you as it is for us.'[10] That same year, the Pope visited Auschwitz and addressed about a million people at Birkenau (where most of the Jews were killed). As he viewed a Hebrew inscription there, he made this statement:

> It is not permissible for anybody to pass by this inscription with indifference ... It is impossible merely to visit it [Auschwitz]. It is necessary on this occasion to think with fear of how far hatred can go, how far man's destruction of man can go, how far cruelty can go.[11]

The following year (1980), John Paul gave an address to the Central Council of Jews in Mainz Germany, a city which was the scene of much persecution since the Middle Ages. On this occasion he encouraged Jews and Christians to get to know each other and each other's faiths and to shed the old caricatures and stereotypes of the past. To the Catholic faithful in particular, he said:

9 Davies, *Europe: A History.*
10 Maher, op. cit.
11 Ibid.

> Christians should aim at understanding better the
> fundamental elements of the religious tradition
> of Judaism, and learn what fundamental lines are
> essential for the religious reality lived by the Jews,
> according to their own understanding.

Quoting this statement from the German Bishops'
'Declaration on the Jews', 'He who encounters Jesus Christ
encounters Judaism', and condemning the theology which
claims that the Covenant of Sinai has been superseded by the
Covenant of the New Testament (replacement theology), he
said:

> The depth and the richness of our common
> heritage are revealed to us particularly in friendly
> dialogue and trusting collaboration ... The first
> dimension of this dialogue, that is the meeting
> between the people of God of the Old Covenant
> never revoked by God and that of the New
> Covenant, is at the same time a dialogue within
> our Church, that is to say, between the first and
> the second part of her Bible ... the second
> dimension of our dialogue ... is the meeting
> between present day Christian Churches and the
> present-day people of the Covenant concluded
> with Moses.[12]

In 1986 the Pope visited Rome's central synagogue, the first
Pope ever to do so. In his address to that assembly he referred
to the Jewish people as 'elder brothers of the Church' and
took the opportunity to acknowledge the acts of
discrimination and oppression that had been done to Jews

12 Ibid.

over the centuries, describing them as 'gravely deplorable manifestations'. He specifically expressed his abhorrence for the genocide committed against the Jewish people during the last war. Drawing attention to the main points of *Nostra aetate*, he reminded his hearers that the Jewish religion is not 'extrinsic' to us (Christians), but in a certain way is 'intrinsic' to our religion, since 'we have a relationship with Judaism that we do not have with any other religion ...'. Pointing out that Christians and Jews have a common responsibility as 'trustees of an ethic marked by the Ten Commandments' and a need to collaborate with each other in this hour when 'society is often lost in agnosticism and individualism', he encouraged positive cooperation between both faiths.[13]

Pope John Paul's teaching and actions in relation to everything to do with the Jews were consistent at all levels. In accordance with his declaration that we need to view the faith of Jews according to their own understanding, and aware of the importance of the state of Israel in the faith understanding of Jews today, he set up diplomatic relations between that State and the Holy See. In 1994 ambassadors were exchanged between the Vatican and Israel.

The issue of the possible bearing of the Christian scriptures on anti-Semitism was a difficult one even for theologians. The Jewish historian already mentioned, Jules Isaac, had studied this subject many years before, setting forth his conclusions in *Jesus et Israel* and John XXIII had opened the way for this study among Catholic theologians. In 1997 Pope John Paul formally asked the Biblical Pontifical Commission to study the roots of Christian anti-Judaism in biblical interpretation. (This body published important new teachings on the subject in 'The Jewish People and their Sacred Scriptures in the Christian Bible' in 2002).

13 Ibid.

Progress had been made but still there had been no apology to the Jewish people. When the document 'We Remember: A Reflection on the Shoah' was issued by the Vatican in 1998, Pope John Paul welcomed it by strengthening its text with a most unusual personal letter. But even this document fell short of making a formal apology and the Jews were disappointed once again. Writing in *The Tablet* a Jewish scholar named Kessler explains their position:

> 'We Remember' speaks of those Christians who helped Jews and those who failed to do so, but implies a balanced picture. It fails to give a plain statement on the role of Christian teachings and stereotypes in motivating those who behaved negatively. Nevertheless it was highly significant, for it acknowledged the Christian contribution to Jewish suffering ... it demonstrated how the Catholic Church, instead of being part of the problem of anti-Semitism, was now becoming part of its solution.[14]

In preparation for the celebration of a Jubilee Year in 2000, the Pope had already called on Catholics to confess the sins of the past with humility and penitence.[15] It was appropriate therefore that the celebrations for the Millennium included a liturgy of repentance in St Peter's in Rome, and that this liturgy included a call (a) for contrition regarding Christian teaching against Jews and Judaism over the centuries, and for the failures of the Church during the Holocaust. This event was followed by the Pope's official visit to Israel where, in the eyes of the whole world, he placed a prayer of repentance in the Western Wall. The text of the prayer was as follows:

14 Edward Kessler (a Jewish scholar), *The Tablet*, 22 October 2005.
15 *Tertio Millennio Adveniente*, 1994.

> God of our fathers, we are deeply saddened by the behaviour of those who, in the course of history, have caused these children of yours to suffer and, asking for your forgiveness, we wish to commit ourselves to genuine brotherhood with the people of the Covenant.

The Pope's visit to Israel was widely reported as a great success. One Israeli cabinet minister is quoted as saying: 'I believe the visit has brought to an end an era of conflict, war and bloodshed between Christians and Jews. We are in a new millennium of reconciliation and peace.'[16]

Speaking at a conference in Rome in October 2005, Rabbi David Rosen explained the power of the two historic visits: to the synagogue in Rome and to Israel:

> I like to use two metaphors to portray the impact on public perception among Israel Jewry. The one is to describe the Jewish people as having had their ears boxed so often in the course of history that their eardrums are damaged to the extent that they are often unable to distinguish between evil sounds and beautiful music. Accordingly, the latter often cannot even be identified when it is being played, especially when it is assumed on the basis of past experience that those playing the instruments only make hostile sounds and continue to do so. However, it is the hearing that has been damaged and not the vision. Thus a new reality can be heard, as it were, only when it can be seen. This, as I have said, was part and parcel of the significance of the Papal visit to the synagogue in Rome in 1986.

16 Maher, op. cit., p. 197.

And this was even more the significance of the Papal visit to Israel when he was seen at the Holocaust memorial in tearful solidarity with Jewish pain and suffering; at the Western Wall in respect for Jewish Tradition and placing there his prayer from the liturgy of repentance that he had conducted in St Peter's shortly beforehand, asking the Divine forgiveness for sins perpetrated by Christians against Jews down the ages.

Indeed, the official State receptions, on arrival, departure and at the President's residence, reflected both recognition and respect for the sovereign Jewish nation re-established in its ancestral homeland.

The second image presented by Dr Rosen was of 'a garden surrounded by high walls which for the overwhelming majority of its history has been an ugly place ... The Papal visit opened up the gates and revealed to many who had not known it, or believed it, the new reality of Catholic-Jewish relations, to discover that the head of the Church himself was in fact a sincere friend of the Jewish people who sought its welfare and mutual respect.' Dr Rosen affirms that it was the Pope's meeting with the Chief Rabbis in Israel on this occasion that opened the way for a permanent committee of the Chief Rabbinate of Israel to dialogue with the Holy See. He says:

The five bilateral meetings so far have exceeded expectations in terms of content and in the personal relationships that have been established, to the degree that this framework is now quite firmly established.

He gives his assessment of all that has happened in these words already quoted: 'a remarkable reckoning of the soul on the part of the Church and its rediscovery of its unique relationship with Judaism and the Jewish people.' In concluding his address, Rabbi Rosen gives us a glimpse of developments in the Jewish community leading to the declaration 'Abru Emet' (Speak the Truth, 2001). Finally he adds, with obvious satisfaction: 'This statement of a Jewish religious reappraisal of Christianity [signed by hundreds of rabbis] received a remarkably warm response from Catholic leaders.'

There are many more questions to be faced by both our faiths in this whole process, but the message of Pope John Paul II, quoted by Dr Rosen at the end of his address, is surely as valid today as it was when first spoken:

> As the children of Abraham we are called, Christians and Jews, to be a blessing to the world. In order to be such, we must be first of all a blessing to one another.[17]

For religious Jews today 'the return to the Land' can only be a miracle. As they consider the number of people involved, the shortness of time between their liberation from the concentration camps and the declaration of the state, and the successful defence of the fledgling state against five Arab countries immediately after, they ask the question, 'How can this be explained in human terms only?' Well may one wonder.

It is also to be observed that what has happened in the Catholic Church since *Nostra aetate* is also outside the normal course of human events. What other organisation of its size and bureaucratic structure has ever declared itself to have been wrong or to have altered a policy hallowed by the passage

17 Dr David Rosen, '"Nostra aetate": Forty Years after Vatican II: Present and Future Perspectives', address given at the Conference of Holy See Commission for Religious Relations with Jewry, Rome, 27 October 2005.

of two thousand years for that reason? Indeed 'a remarkable reckoning of the soul on the part of the Church' has taken place. We remind the reader of the following quotes included at the beginning of this book:

> The schism within the Judeo-Christian tradition has been generated on both sides by intense feelings of betrayal ... It is an unresolved and irresolvable quarrel within the family ...

> Notwithstanding the doctrine of forgiveness, it is the hardest thing in the world to see themselves as partners in the same tradition. Only the most Christian of Christians can contemplate calling the Jews 'our elder brethren'...

This judgement takes no account, however, of 'the miracle of repentance' spoken of above by Rabbi Heschel, our Jewish brother.

Ireland has never had a large Jewish community and that may be why our intolerance, as some have observed, has focused more on other Christian denominations. We may not have a record of centuries of vicious pogroms but, sadly, history shows that we are no different than our fellow Europeans when the occasion arises. We too are called therefore to a serious 'reckoning of soul'. It is the contention of this study that the first step in this process is to become well informed. Truthfulness and repentance alone can bring about genuine reconciliation between us and our Jewish brethren. This reconciliation, in the words of Pope John Paul II and his immediate predecessors, is also the prerequisite for reconciliation between us and other Christian denominations, the absence of which has been the cause of so much division in our national history and is a constant hindrance to the spread of the Gospel.

For us Catholics then, Pope John Paul II has taken the lead. It is our responsibility to enter wholeheartedly into this 'change of heart' and so give to our world the message of hope that it longs for: 'Peace on earth to all who are of good will.'

Extract from Obituary of Sr Rose Thering OP

Sr Rose Thering, the American nun whose pioneering work on Catholic anti-Semitism contributed to the Second Vatican Council's emphasis on closer relations between the Church and Judaism, died on 6 May at a convent in her native Wisconsin. She was eighty-five.

As a child on a Midwestern dairy farm, Rose Thering recalled that the only Jews she knew were in her catechetical textbooks. Her family and others, however, held to the belief, still propagated in Church teaching at the time, that the Jewish race was collectively responsible for the crucifixion of Jesus.

After entering the Sisters of St Dominic and becoming a school teacher, she examined the textbooks further and found that their commentary on Jews made her 'ill'. The revulsion inspired the cause to which she devoted the rest of her life. Her doctoral dissertation at St Louis University, which explored the Church's stated teachings on Judaism and other faiths, was cited as a significant element of the drafting of *Nostra aetate*, the Second Vatican Council decree that repudiated the prior charge against the Jewish people and declared that 'the Church ... decries hatred, persecutions, displays of anti-Semitism, directed against Jews at any time and by anyone'.

Her dissertation was taken to the Council by Rabbi Marc Tannenbaum and presented to the American bishops.

According to the president of the International Council for Christians and Jews, Fr John Pawlikowskiu, *Nostra aetate* was in danger of being defeated but it was rescued by the American bishops 'who all voted for it'. (Rocco Palmo, *The Tablet*, Summer 2006)

Extracts from *Healing the Wounds of History* by Monsignor Peter Hocken[1]

Repenting for the Sins of the Past

The call for Catholics to confess the sins of the past is something new in Catholic history. It was first expressed in 1994 by Pope John Paul II in his letter *Tertio Millennio Adveniente* (*TMA*), initiating the Church's preparation for the Great Jubilee of the year 2000.

Next a document entitled 'Memory and Reconciliation: The Church and the Faults of the Past' (*MR*), containing the theological reflection of the International Theological Commission, was published a few days before the penitential liturgy celebrated in St Peter's Rome, on 12 March 2000. (As part of this liturgy – presided over by the Pope himself – seven prelates from key offices in the Roman Curia confessed sins relating in some way to the area of their responsibilities.)

From 1994 on, John Paul II took a number of opportunities to acknowledge a Catholic responsibility for sins of the past, especially during his visit to Israel in 2000 and his visit to Athens in 2001.

Why is a Christian repentance happening at this time in history?

Perhaps because today the conflicts that are tearing the human race apart threaten the future of all humanity.

1   London: Goodnews, 2005.

Through the mass media, we cannot be unaware of the appalling barbarities that are being committed in so many parts of the world. It shocks us that such horrors occur also in supposedly Christian nations at a time when we prided ourselves on our scientific and technological progress. Above all, the slaughter of six million Jews in the Holocaust has provoked a radical examination of the Christian conscience: how could such a horror have happened in Christian Europe?

(a)   The Holy Father's conviction reflects both his life-long reflection on the major evils of the twentieth century, through which he himself had lived in Poland, coupled with his sense of the year 2000 presenting a historic opportunity for the Church and for the world.

(b)   Pope John Paul saw this call for a Catholic confession of the sins of the past as a fruit of the Second Vatican Council, an essential element in the renewal of the Church, and as necessary for the effectiveness of the 'new evangelisation'.

Protestant Church leaders have also understood that the deep wounds, resulting from past conflicts, constitute a major barrier to the effective evangelisation of our peoples.

Therefore the attention of Christians, both Protestant and Catholic, is being directed towards the root causes of the long standing conflicts that continue to plague peoples and nations throughout the world.

Since all Christians recognise that repentance and reconciliation cannot happen apart from the Spirit of God, this new awareness of the need to address and to confess the sins of the past should be understood as a *kairos* in the biblical sense, *a decisive turning point in history.*

Pope John Paul's Distinctive Contribution: Purification of Memories

(a)   The first contribution of John Paul II is to have placed this issue on the Church's agenda. What is clearly new today is the Pope's presentation of the confession of past sins as a *task for the whole Church* to undertake.

(b)   The Holy Father identified the purpose of this confession of past sins as *'purification of memory'*. This concept is a major Catholic contribution to the understanding of what it means to confess the sins of the past.

The Holy Father (in *TMA*) singled out two patterns of past sin that particularly need to be confessed:

(1)   sins against the unity of God's People;

(2)   sins of 'intolerance and even the use of violence in the service of truth'.

(It is clear from the Pope's actions that the sins of Catholics against the Jewish people have weighed heavily on his heart and played a major role in the call for repentance.)

'Purification (of memory) aims at liberating *personal* and *communal* conscience from all forms of resentment and violence that are the legacy of past faults.'(*MR*)

(1)   In times of violence and brutality the most dangerous memories are the *communal memories* i.e. the way that a people or community remembers its conflicts, writes its history, identifies its enemies, and justifies its own behaviour.

(2)   Because all these 'communal memories' are accompanied and fuelled by 'personal memories' – stories of particular families and individuals with their own sufferings and traumas – these memories are then handed down to the following generations, not only in official histories, but also in popular culture: in songs,

art, days of special remembrance that have their own ceremonies and processions, the honouring of 'our heroes'.

If we take recent examples such as former Yugoslavia, Northern Ireland, Rwanda and Sri Lanka we find that in each of these cases the histories of the opposing sides have little in common except that: 'We are the heroes and they are the villains.'

Such conflicts then can never be healed without a purification of memories that is without being purified from the bias and lies in the accounts of our histories. This purification in turn purifies our hearts from hatred and rejection of each other.

The *Catechism* [*of the Catholic Church*] tells us that: 'The Holy Spirit is the Church's living memory' (1099).

The purification of memory requires a separation of truth from untruth in our memories. Therefore we need recourse to the Holy Spirit who (1) enables and empowers the recalling of God's works; (2) convicts us of the sins of the past; and (3) convicts us also of all distortions of truth.

But surely we are only responsible for our own sins? How can we repent of sins we did not commit? True, we are only responsible to God for our own behaviour but: 'While no man is responsible for what his ancestors have done, he *is* responsible for what he does with that memory.' (Elie Weisel)

The Church and Sin

Since the Church in the fullest sense includes Christ, the head, and all the Church triumphant with Mary and all the saints, we can in no way impute sin to the Church in this deepest sense.

But the Decree on Ecumenism [*Unitatis Redintegratio* (*UR*)] speaks of the Church militant when it says: 'Christ summons the Church, as she goes on her pilgrim way, to that continual reform of which she always has need, insofar as she is a human institution here on earth' (*UR*, 6).

Pope Adrian VI in 1522 spoke of: 'the abominations, the abuses ... and the lies' of which the Roman Curia of his time was guilty, 'deep-rooted and extensive ... sickness', extending 'from the top to the members'. (*MR*)

A sinful element does exist in the Church *and* it is not confined to individuals. There is a corporate dimension to the sins of Catholics, from which even the hierarchy cannot *a priori* be excluded. For example, it could be that the Bishop's Conference of a particular nation is led to confess their sin as a body in not addressing in honesty and faith the issue of child abuse at the hands of servants of the Church.

To say that: 'the Church has not sinned, it's only some Catholics ...' is not convincing to people reading about scandalous situations in the Church and the slow response of Church authorities to such scandalous situations e.g. to child abuse. For the general public, this is the Church. For this reason it is an urgent pastoral requirement to be able to speak of the sinful aspect of the Church as a human institution, without losing sight of the deeper theological reality of the Church.

The Pope's appeal for a confession of the sins of Catholics in the past must not then be thought of in an individualistic way only. It has both personal and corporate dimensions.

(1)   When we are dealing with grave patterns of sin from centuries ago, we are hardly ever dealing just with the sins of particular people, even particular leaders; generally we are dealing with attitudes and practices that characterised groups, nations and even the whole Church militant over generations.

(2)   Solidarity among the baptised is another reason for this kind of repentance: 'Indeed, in grace and in the woundedness of sin the baptised of today are close to, and in solidarity with, those of yesterday' (*MR*, 3).

Protestant initiatives in the area of reconciliation have focused on identifying with his/her own people or nation. Catholics will want to add to this the divisions and wounds of the churches and the different Christian communities.

The biblical basis for *identification* is found in the prophetic confession: 'We and our fathers have sinned' and the great examples are Nehemiah and Daniel. In chapter 9 of both books, we find a long confession of the sins of the fathers, accompanied by a confession of the sins of their own generation. Maybe this simple biblical confession, 'we and our fathers have sinned', shows us Catholics how to confess the sins of our people in a theologically acceptable way.

The concept of identification is important. It means that the person making the confession identifies with his/her ancestors. The 'we' refers to both the present and the past. 'Our' ancestors committed these sins, 'our' people turned away from the Lord. In Nehemiah 9:2 we read: 'Then those of Israelite lineage separated themselves from all foreigners; and they stood and confessed their sins and the iniquities of their fathers.' A major teacher on reconciliation, John Dawson, notes of this incident that: 'They completely identified with their nation and its history.'

Note that our redemption has been accomplished by such an act of identification – by the One who was innocent and free of all sin. The model for understanding this need to 'identify with and repent of' the sins of our fathers is Jesus himself. The Gospel of Matthew presents the baptism of Jesus in the Jordan in this way. John the Baptist sees the obvious inappropriateness – according to ordinary human thinking – of his baptising the sinless Jesus: 'I need to be baptised by you, and do you come to me?' (Mt 3:14). But Jesus replies: 'Let it be so now; it is proper for us to do this to fulfil all righteousness' (Mt 3:15). Jesus so identifies with all sinners that he takes the consequences of all sin upon himself. The fulfilment of this identification in the cross of Calvary accomplishes the righteousness of God.

Jesus also recognises *solidarity in sin over generations*, in his warnings against the scribes and Pharisees (Matthew 23) and when he bluntly says: 'Thus you witness against yourselves, that you are sons of those who murdered the prophets' (v.31).

Initiatives

Official initiatives of identificational repentance take place when people in authority who officially represent their nation or Church confess the sins of their ancestors, identify with them and ask forgiveness. This governmental level of repentance has to be made as public as possible since the participants are officially representing their entire people. However, such public occasions are not suited to deep grieving, and if they are to be effective, the way needs to be prepared by the private and *unofficial* initiatives of Christians led by the Holy Spirit.

The Process of Reconciliation

Four elements are needed.

1. Research: We must 'get the facts right'. This is all the more necessary when people from both sides of an historical conflict are praying together. The goal is that all present at such intercessory prayer can say 'Amen' to the confession of the sin and the assertions about past history. We will endanger the whole process if we make false historical statements.

2. Confession: We have to discern between the good and the evil. The confession of past sins involves saying: 'This happened in the past. And it was evil.' It is wise to focus on the most blatant evils. It is essential too that the acknowledgment of past acts as evil does not descend into judgement of particular people.

3. Identification: This means that we identify with those who perpetrated the sins or evils being confessed. It means moving from 'They' to 'We' to affirm the spiritual link through folk-memory between the generations of the past and our generation today. It is possible to identify with groups or nations to which we do not belong, in order to confess their past sins because Jesus as a Jew identified with all peoples of the earth. Identification with another group, church or people, however, cannot just be an intercessory technique. It has to be a personal commitment to the others – as missionaries who follow the example of Jesus and take on the culture of the people they serve.

4. Lamentation: To complete the process there must be a grieving heart. The key principle is that *effective repentance requires a sorrow for sin as deep as the emotional and personal involvement of those who committed the atrocities of the past*. When we are dealing with brutal events involving evils such as massacres, torture, rape, enforced exile (what we now call ethnic cleansing), humiliation and degradation, we have to realise that hatred and contempt consumed the perpetrators. Little that is significant will be achieved until the repentance goes as deep as the sin. But such a grieving of heart cannot be planned or orchestrated. It requires a seeking of the Lord to allow the Holy Spirit to show us the real horror of the sin before the all-holy God. This normally belongs to the sphere of unofficial non-publicised meetings. The charismatic renewal is making an important contribution here – the Lord (through the renewal) is enabling us to reconnect with our hearts and to express profound emotions in our prayer and worship.

5. Forgiveness: Forgiveness is not a major focus in *MR*. Fundamentally, the need (a) to confess and to repent

for the sins of the past, and (b) the need for our memories to be purified, is not dependent on asking for forgiveness or receiving it. Forgiveness belongs to the *response* to confessions of sin – their response to our confession and our response to their confession. But forgiveness must always be asked of God. For all sin is first of all an offence against God. This applies to all confessions of past sins, whether official or unofficial, public or hidden.

When seeking forgiveness of each other we need to be sensitive to the dispositions of the victim-group. Descendants of people offended against in the past may not feel that they have the right or the capacity to grant forgiveness. This is often the case with Jewish people who will usually say that forgiveness is in the hands of God, and the only humans who could grant it are dead.

Secondly we should be sensitive also to the depth of the past suffering and avoid trivialising the evils of the past by thinking that we can enter fully into their history after reading a few books and spending a few hours in prayer.

Conclusion

It would seem that the Holy Spirit is teaching the Church about 'identificational repentance' and the purification of memories at this time and that the Spirit's timing is connected with the gravity of the world situation in which we live. It shows the depth of the renewal that the Father of mercies is willing for the Church and the world.

The first need for us is to understand. Only then can we teach. As we respond to the Spirit's call for a confession of the sins of the past, we are contributing in a significant way to the renewal of the Church and the evangelisation of the world.

Acknowledgements

In Irish we say, *'Is ar scáth a chéile a mhaireann na daoine'*, meaning that we depend on each other and cannot 'go it alone'. Perhaps one of the greatest ways to learn this is to write a book. There are so many people (and groups of people) who deserve my thanks for their time, moral support, criticism, and above all their prayer. These special friends know who they are and I hope that, if I do not mention them personally, they will nonetheless accept the fact that I am deeply grateful to them all.

It would not be right, however, to omit an explicit 'thank you' to the following: Joan O'Donovan OP, who was the first to give me the necessary encouragement to publish this document; to Paddy Monaghan, whose moral support was crucial, especially after the rejection of my first effort, and who gave the necessary guidance that enabled me to turn my mistakes around; to Patrick Kanaiah, who laboriously typed along as I experimented with this phrase or that, and gave such encouragement to persevere at the task. The prayer support of St Micheal's Prayer Group, Dun Laoire, cannot be measured; the practical help of my sister Cora and my brother Michael, who took over when I couldn't face another trawl through the book in search of necessary corrections. Eugene Boyle, who as well as giving enormous encouragement also undertook to painstakingly prepare the book for a publisher; the librarians, Teresa (Catholic Central Library) and Slaine

(Irish School of Ecumenics), both of whom gave such generous help to this total stranger; and thanks to two of the most faithful friends one could hope to have: Marie Fidgeon and Eleanor Canterbury of Wicklow, who were always there to encourage and support. My deepest thanks to all of you. I would like also to express my thanks to Maura Hyland and her team at Veritas who have been so helpful and so easily accessible whenever I needed them. *Go gcúití Dia sibh go leir.*